THIS IS A COOKBOOK

MAX SUSSMAN + ELI SUSSMAN

PHOTOGRAPHY ALEX FARNUM

ILLUSTRATIONS DIANA HEOM

Lazy Brunch

PAGE 15 →

Brunch should be an official American holiday. For us, it's a weekly tradition that encourages sleeping in late, eating in pajamas, day drinking, and slathering butter, syrup, gravy, and jam across every inch of your plate. If you host pot-luck style, you'll be stocked with leftovers for the week and in close proximity to your couch for the rest of the day.

Backyard Grub

↓ PAGE 33

For summertime nirvana, all you need are good drinks, some quality meat, and a spot to grill. Identify someone you know with a pool, then ingratiate yourself by offering what they most need: meat for grilling and booze for drinking. Bring over the grub and a 12-pack every time and you'll be golden. No friend with a pool? Make nice with whomever you can find with a great yard, roof deck, patio, or lake access.

Night In

← PAGE 57

We're just going to come out and say it: This chapter is about sex. Yes, it's about food too, but if you've decided to invite someone over to cook dinner—just you and that one person—your goal probably isn't to nail the dish perfectly. And regardless of your kitchen skills, it becomes a win-win—make good food, and you're the sexy chef; ruin the recipe, and you're the adorable gave-it-your-all cook. Your date is already in your apartment, which takes care of navigating through the awkward car goodbye. Basically what we are saying is—if you can't make this work, you are hopeless.

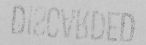

Dinner Party

PAGE 85 →

Your first dinner party may have dissolved into a full-blown rager instead of being the classy "adult" affair you dreamt up. But like a fine wine (and not 2-Buck Chuck), your dinner parties will get better over time. These are our go-to recipes for having a group of people over. Don't overthink it, or waste time trying to channel Martha Stewart. None of your friends give a shit about napkin holders. Just keep it simple, have your guests bring the booze, and put on some Motown. People will be begging you to host again.

Midnight Snacks

**PAGE 123**

We're really hungry when we get off work after midnight and often looking for that certain something to hold us over before heading out drinking, collapsing in front of the laptop, or crawling into bed. These snacks can be made any time of day, but the point is these recipes are fast and use ingredients you probably have lying around. So if you need to eat RIGHT NOW, these recipes are where it's at.

Sweet Stuff

**PAGE 141** →

It seems like every food reality TV show is about a bakery. (Who knew there was so much drama involved in baking cupcakes?) But it makes sense. When tempted properly with the right option, everyone is able to make room for dessert. If you're looking for something crazy decadent and rich, or a lighter fruitier option, we've put together some of our favorites. And coming from two guys who would take another piece of meat over a slice of cake any day, that's saying a lot.

rob delaney
FOREWORD

What do you most look forward to when you get up in the morning? Going back to bed as soon as possible? Me too. I have a California king bed and man, it's like a cozy little spaceship where I'm the cozy little spaceboss. The second thing I look forward to is eating. And when I say "eating," I don't mean mere sustenance. I mean I like to push my stomach's needle into the red and strain my pants' suspension. Did I mention I'm part car? Well guess what? It's 2012 and cars eat ham now, so shut up. While I may be a glutton, I'm a discerning glutton. I've lived in New York, Paris, or Los Angeles my whole adult life and my taste buds have matured sexily.

Over the last few years I've taken up cooking for myself, my family, and anyone else who isn't afraid to watch me eat. And since anything worth doing is worth doing well, especially if it's going in your mouth, I'm excited about this book. I've deemed it worthy of the title The Belly Bible. (Ed. Note: Everyone, including the authors, felt this was a very bad idea.)

It's common knowledge that cooking and eating are dangerous; people die every day cooking and/or eating. That's why you need a guide to help you in your kitchen. With the Sussmans, you get two guides, so you're actually half as likely to die with this cookbook as you would be with any other cookbook. And the Sussmans are brothers, who probably sleep in their mom's pantry in bunk beds made out of big cheese wheels and salami. But that's their business; what we do know is that they're good at designing ridiculously tasty meals that are easy to prepare, even if you're stupid, drunk, or Maroon 5.

Flip through this book—without eating it—and take a look at the grilled meatball sandwich, the pulled pork, and the chocolate-peanut butter pie. Look at the simplicity of the recipes. You want it, don't you? OK—you can lick it. Lick the book. I won't tell. Once you're done licking the book, use it. Make these dishes and eat them. You'll be happy you did.

THE Sussmans are brothers, who probably sleep in their mom's PANTRY IN BUNK BEDS made out of big cheese wheels and salami.

introduction

We'll be totally honest with you—we are completely, unabashedly obsessed with food. We even have a chalkboard in our apartment to keep a running list of restaurants we want to try. One of us has food ordering nightmares and the other has delusional daydreams of creating the world's greatest sandwich. Food runs our professional and personal lives (debating where to go to eat on our days off often dissolves into courtroom-style drama with deliberation and each side providing evidence) and, truly, we wouldn't want it any other way.

We're all about experiencing the unknown, and trying new foods is our favorite way to learn about other cultures. We totally get that some people aren't super-adventurous and may need a push to try new foods. This cookbook is that push away from frozen food lunches and dinners from a national chain. This book is going to show you how to cook new ethnic dishes, try a flavor combination you've avoided, and learn new techniques you've only witnessed on TV.

Everyone likes to be fed and cooking is a vital skill to have. Taking stand-alone ingredients and transforming them into a cohesive dish is an ability that will never cease to blow peoples' minds. We've taken everything we've learned in our 10+ years of cooking and simplified it big time. Our book is going to help you create straightforward and tasty food for your girlfriend/boyfriend, for a group of friends, or just for yourself.

Don't let a small kitchen be an excuse (we recipe tested and photographed 45 dishes for this book using two little burners). If there's enough space for you to stand in the kitchen, you can cook this entire book. We've done it all—putting a cutting board over the sink, using a garbage can as a shelf, stacking spices to the ceiling—and we'll share every trick and bit of knowledge we've acquired with you. So having this book is almost as good as having us by your side in the kitchen.

Whatever you've avoided until now—grilling, braising, reducing a sauce, making pasta from scratch—the only way to get good at it is to try. If you're afraid of burning food, you'll never learn. If you think you're only a "fast food" or "American food" person, stop being so boring. And if you say you just can't do it, well, you're just flat out wrong. So turn the page, and get cooking.

Max & Eli

WHAT WE LIKE TO COOK

max I like to cook real food that tastes good. Seasonal stuff that's not too fancy. A lot of meat and vegetables. I like to just go to the store without a plan or recipe in mind and buy something interesting and figure out how to put it together in a meal. It's fun to pick out a few good-looking ingredients then come up with new ways to bring them together.

eli I like to cook stuff for myself that people would find at a diner or deli. Simple classics like chicken salad or club sandwiches, garlic mashed potatoes, stir fry with rice, or fast pasta dishes made from gathering any vegetables in the fridge, sautéeing them up, and it's ready. I also like making French fries in the oven. They are awesome with a sandwich, a steak, or meatloaf. Meat, bread, and pasta are definitely my go-tos. If it's a homey-style dish that doesn't take much time, that's what I'm gonna cook for myself.

in the BEGINNING

eli Our first cooking job together was at our childhood summer camp. Max was the chef. One night he left me in charge of the kitchen and I burned the soup that was supposed to feed something like 200 people. I scorched the bottom about 10 minutes before dinner started. It sucked. We quickly threw together some leftovers and most people ate peanut butter and jelly sandwiches. It was a gross dinner and people were pretty annoyed at me. That was a huge eye-opening experience. I remember it every time I cook now because I never want to be the guy who burns soup (or anything) again.

max That was the same summer that it took the entire time to figure out how to cook rice. One week, it was burnt. The next week, it was watery and cold. Every week it was something. How do you cook rice for 200 people without a rice cooker? We kept trying. We tried a different technique every week. We finally got it. The feeling when you figure out something like that is amazing. It's the closest you can get to the feeling of winning a wizard fight—like you've just conquered your ancient nemesis.

eli The good thing is that you learn from messing up and make sure that you never do it again, so that works in your favor.

max Anyone who's more skilled than you are in the kitchen has made all the same mistakes plus a lot more. So to get better, you have to go through that, too. We're here to help pave the way for you.

eli There are always going to be things that don't come together that well and mistakes will get made. (I've definitely fallen asleep while making chicken nuggets and almost burned down the house.) But even when a dish comes out great, there's always something we could do to make it even better the next time. We are still learning, too, and working to get better every day.

WHY we (can) COOK

max We grew up in a family where food and cooking were really important. I learned early on from my mom that the act of cooking and then eating is just as important as the food you're preparing. The whole point is to bring people together. Growing up, we had a family dinner almost every night. Cooking became something I would do in my spare time to be creative, and then I started working in restaurants.

eli My first cooking job was at the Detroit Zoo food court. I ran the grill. It meant a crazy amount of burgers on the grill for hours and hours straight in sweltering heat. Hundreds of crying kids and screaming parents and everyone wanting their burger five minutes ago. It was an AWESOME first cooking job.

max One of my first cooking jobs was in a macrobiotic vegetarian restaurant making salads. Then I cooked at the law school snack bar making grilled cheese sandwiches, and I also delivered pizzas. I've done everything from making corned beef at a Jewish deli, and cooking mussels at a fine dining place in Ann Arbor, to roasting a whole lamb over an open fire at a fishing lodge in South America. I've worked every station.

eli These days I work the line at a restaurant in Brooklyn. I'm constantly learning there and have picked up a ton from Max. We've recently done a couple of pig roasts together. I just keep a close eye on what everyone is doing. Surrounding yourself with people who have more experience is the best way to get better. With our book, we're helping you learn from our mistakes and lean on our experience. You can steal all the cool stuff we've picked up over the years and use it in your own kitchen.

ROLL OUT OF BED
AND PUT ON A MOTOWN
RECORD. IT'S TIME
FOR EGGS AND DAY
DRINKING.

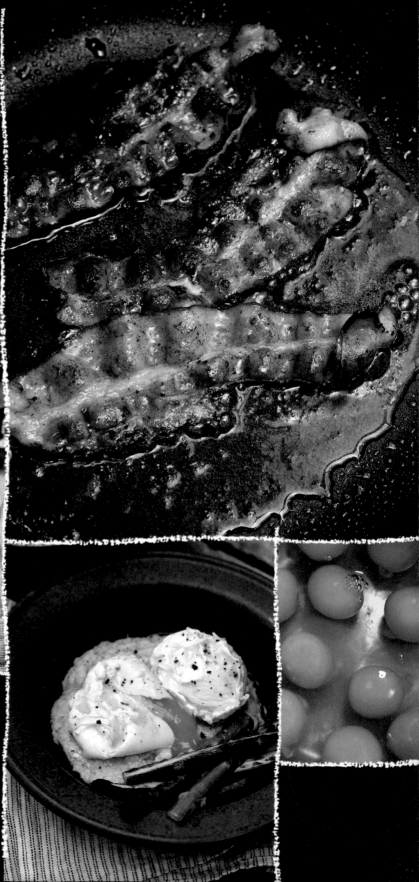

Lazy Brunch

BREAKFAST OF MONTE CRISTO 16

CHILAQUILES WITH TOMATILLO SALSA 19

FRIED CHICKEN AND WAFFLES 20

BUTTERMILK BISCUITS WITH CHORIZO GRAVY 21

LATKES WITH LOTS OF SAUCES 22

MAKIN' BACON PROJECT 24

CHEESY POLENTA WITH POACHED EGGS AND SAUTÉED ASPARAGUS 27

ONION, GRUYÈRE, AND POTATO TART 28

TURKISH BAKED EGGS 30

NUTELLA BUNS 31

IT'S A LITTLE-KNOWN LITERARY FACT THAT
DURING THE 14 YEARS EDMOND DANTÈS SPENT
AT CHÂTEAU D'IF, HE WAS DRIVEN TO SURVIVE **NOT**
BY HIS DESIRE TO EXACT REVENGE ON FERNAND,
DANGLARS, AND VILLEFORT. IN REALITY HE
JUST REALLY WANTED TO EAT THIS SANDWICH.

BREAKFAST of monte CRISTO

4 LARGE EGGS

¼ CUP (2 FL OZ/60 ML)
HEAVY CREAM

1 TSP SALT

1 TSP SUGAR

4 ENGLISH MUFFINS, SPLIT

4 THIN SLICES
GRUYÈRE CHEESE

4 THICK OR 8 THIN SLICES
SMOKED HAM

DIJON MUSTARD
TO TASTE

3 TBSP UNSALTED BUTTER

YOUR FAVORITE JAM,
PURE MAPLE SYRUP,
AND/OR POWDERED
SUGAR FOR SERVING

1. Preheat the oven to 350°F (180°C).

2. In a large bowl, whisk together the eggs, cream, salt, and sugar. Add the English muffin halves to the batter and let soak for about 10 minutes, turning halfway through.

3. To assemble a sandwich, lift a muffin half from the batter, letting the excess fall back into the bowl, and place on a plate, cut side down. Lay a cheese slice on top of the muffin, followed by 1 or 2 slices of ham. Top the ham with a small dollop of mustard. Place another English muffin half on top, cut side up. Repeat to make the rest of the sandwiches.

4. In a large ovenproof frying pan over medium heat, melt half of the butter. Carefully arrange the assembled sandwiches in the pan and cook until the bottoms are lightly browned, about 3 minutes. Add the remaining butter and let melt, tilting the pan to spread the butter around the pan bottom. Using a wide spatula, turn the sandwiches. Transfer the pan to the oven and bake until the cheese is melted and bubbly, about 10 minutes, turning the sandwiches once again halfway through. Serve right away. Pass your favorite jam, maple syrup, and/or powdered sugar at the table.

YOU ARE HUNGOVER. YOU HAVE CHIPS. YOU
WANT TO EAT SOME BREAKFAST. WE HAVE THE
SOLUTION. CONTINUE READING BELOW.

CHILAQUILES
with
Tomatillo salsa

SERVES 4

FOR THE TOMATILLO SALSA

3 LB (1.5 KG) TOMATILLOS

½ YELLOW ONION,
CUT INTO BIG CHUNKS

1 JALAPEÑO

2 GARLIC CLOVES

2 TBSP
EXTRA-VIRGIN OLIVE OIL

SALT

LEAVES FROM 1 BUNCH
FRESH CILANTRO,
ROUGHLY CHOPPED

4 LARGE EGGS

2 TBSP OLIVE OIL
(OPTIONAL)

2 CUPS (12 OZ/375 G)
LEFTOVER OR STORE-
BOUGHT ROASTED
CHICKEN, SHREDDED
(OPTIONAL)

1 LARGE BAG TORTILLA
CHIPS, PREFERABLY
THICK-CUT

CRUMBLED QUESO FRESCO
FOR SERVING

1. To make the tomatillo salsa, preheat the oven to 400°F (200°C). Peel the papery husks off the tomatillos and rinse under warm water to remove the sticky coating. Put the tomatillos in a large bowl along with the onion, jalapeño, garlic, extra-virgin olive oil, and salt to taste. Toss to mix well. Spread in a single layer on a baking sheet and roast until the skins of the tomatillos and jalapeño are blistered and tender, 20–25 minutes. Let cool slightly, then remove the stem from the jalapeño, along with some or all of the seeds if you want a milder salsa. Transfer the jalapeño and the rest of the contents of the baking sheet to a food processor and process to a coarse purée. Transfer to a bowl and let cool, then stir in half of the cilantro. Taste and adjust the seasoning. Set aside.

2. In a large sauté pan, warm the olive oil over medium heat. Carefully crack the eggs into the pan without breaking the yolks. Cook, without disturbing, until the whites are just set, about 5 minutes. (This is called sunny-side up eggs.)

3. To assemble the chilaquiles, warm the tomatillo salsa and the chicken, if using, in a saucepan until the salsa is just simmering. Spread the chips on a serving platter and arrange a layer of the salsa and chicken, if using, on top. Sprinkle with some crumbled queso fresco and half of the remaining cilantro. Carefully slide the fried eggs on top. Garnish with more queso fresco and cilantro and serve right away.

FOR THE LAZY BRUNCHER THERE'S OFTEN A "CAN'T DECIDE" MOMENT
BETWEEN SWEET OR SAVORY, SO WE GIVE YOU CHICKEN AND WAFFLES,
A BIT OF BREAKFAST AND A BIT OF DINNER. IF YOU'VE NEVER HAD IT, YOU'LL
SOON UNDERSTAND WHY THERE IS AN ENTIRE RESTAURANT CHAIN BUILT
UPON THE FOUNDATION OF THIS COMBO'S DELICIOUSNESS.

FRiED Chicken and waffles

SERVES 6

FOR THE CHICKEN

1 QT (1 L) BUTTERMILK

SALT AND FRESHLY GROUND
BLACK PEPPER

2 TSP CAYENNE PEPPER

1 WHOLE CHICKEN,
3–4 LB (1.5–2 KG),
CUT INTO 6 PIECES

3 QT (3 L) VEGETABLE OIL

4 CUPS (20 OZ/625 G)
ALL-PURPOSE FLOUR

FOR THE WAFFLES

2 CUPS (10 OZ/315 G)
ALL-PURPOSE FLOUR

2 TBSP SUGAR

1 TSP BAKING POWDER

½ TSP BAKING SODA

3 LARGE EGGS, SEPARATED

1½ CUPS (12 FL OZ/375 ML)
WHOLE MILK

4 TBSP (2 OZ/60 G)
UNSALTED BUTTER,
MELTED AND COOLED

PURE MAPLE SYRUP
FOR SERVING

1. To make the chicken, in a large bowl, stir together the buttermilk, 1 Tbsp salt, and the cayenne. Add the chicken pieces and nudge to submerge in the mixture. Cover and refrigerate for at least 2 hours or up to overnight.

2. When ready to fry, in a stockpot, heat the oil over medium heat until it reaches 350°F (180°C) on a deep-frying thermometer. In a large bowl, whisk together the flour, 2 tsp salt, and 1 tsp black pepper. Remove the chicken from the buttermilk mixture, shake off the excess, and place in the flour mixture. Toss to coat well. Using tongs, carefully lower the chicken into the hot oil. Fry, turning as needed, until the chicken is cooked through and the coating is golden brown on all sides, about 12 minutes total. Drain on paper towels and season while still warm. Keep warm in a low oven.

3. To make the waffles, in a large bowl, whisk together the flour, sugar, baking powder, baking soda, and 1 tsp salt. In a medium bowl, beat the egg yolks with the milk and melted butter. In a third bowl, using an electric mixer set on high speed, beat the egg whites until soft peaks form. Pour the milk mixture into the flour mixture and stir until just barely blended and still lumpy. Pour the egg whites over the top and, using a rubber spatula, fold together until just blended. Preheat a waffle iron. Ladle in about ½ cup (4 fl oz/125 ml) batter and cook until crisp and golden. Transfer to a platter and keep warm in the oven while you make the rest of the waffles.

4. Divide the chicken and waffles amongst 6 plates, pour maple syrup over the top of everything, and serve right away.

Buttermilk biscuits with CHORIZO GRAVY

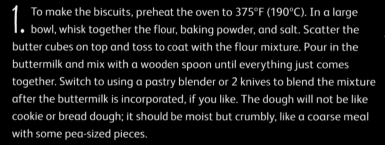

SERVES 4

EVERY FRIDAY MORNING ON A QUIET STREET IN ANN ARBOR, MICHIGAN, VOLUNTEERS AND A ROTATING CAST OF CHEFS TURN A HOME INTO A RESTAURANT CALLED SELMA CAFÉ, WHICH PRIDES ITSELF ON USING ALL LOCAL INGREDIENTS, RIGHT DOWN TO THE FLOUR. WE OFTEN COOKED THERE, AND WHEN WE FEATURED THIS DISH, IT WAS A HUGE HIT. IT'S BEEN A STAPLE FOR US EVER SINCE.

FOR THE BISCUITS

2½ CUPS (12½ OZ/390 G) ALL-PURPOSE FLOUR, SIFTED, PLUS MORE FOR DUSTING

2 TBSP BAKING POWDER

1½ TSP SALT

2 STICKS (1 CUP/8 OZ/250 G) COLD UNSALTED BUTTER, CUT INTO SMALL CUBES

1¼ CUPS (10 FL OZ/310 ML) BUTTERMILK

CHORIZO GRAVY (PAGE 152), WARMED

½ CUP (1½ OZ/45 G) SLICED GREEN ONIONS

½ CUP (½ OZ/15 G) PACKED FRESH CILANTRO LEAVES

1. To make the biscuits, preheat the oven to 375°F (190°C). In a large bowl, whisk together the flour, baking powder, and salt. Scatter the butter cubes on top and toss to coat with the flour mixture. Pour in the buttermilk and mix with a wooden spoon until everything just comes together. Switch to using a pastry blender or 2 knives to blend the mixture after the buttermilk is incorporated, if you like. The dough will not be like cookie or bread dough; it should be moist but crumbly, like a coarse meal with some pea-sized pieces.

2. Turn the dough out onto a generously floured work surface. Lightly flour your hands and push the dough into a mound, then gently work it into a rectangle about 2 inches (5 cm) thick. Continue to flour your work surface and hands as needed to prevent sticking.

3. Fold the dough rectangle in half to make a rough square, then push it gently back into a rectangle, again dusting your hands and work surface with flour as needed to prevent sticking. Repeat this gentle kneading 5 times, then pat the final rectangle to a thickness of about 1½ inches (4 cm). Using a biscuit cutter, a ring mold, or the rim of a pint glass, cut out the biscuits. Pat the scraps together and cut out as many more biscuits as you can. Discard the remaining dough scraps.

4. Arrange the biscuits on a baking sheet, spacing them evenly. Bake until the tops are lightly golden, 35–40 minutes, rotating the baking sheet halfway through.

5. To serve, arrange 2 biscuits on each of 4 plates and ladle the warm chorizo gravy over the top. Garnish with the green onions and cilantro and serve right away.

OUR DAD MAKES THESE EVERY YEAR ON HANUKKAH.
AND HE MAKES A HUGE MESS. HE PUTS NEWSPAPERS ON THE FLOOR,
USES EVERY BURNER, AND THE WHOLE HOUSE SMELLS BAD FOR
A WEEK. BUT THEY ARE SUPER DELICIOUS AND WE HAD TO INCLUDE
THEM IN OUR BOOK. WE MAKE THEM ALMOST EVERY WEEKEND.
WE HAD OUR DAD TEST THE RECIPE.

SERVES 4-6

FOR THE LOX SAUCE

1 CUP (8 OZ/250 G)
SOUR CREAM

3 OZ (90 G) LOX, DICED

1 TBSP MINCED FRESH CHIVES

FOR THE APPLESAUCE

1 CUP (9 OZ/280 G)
APPLESAUCE

1 TBSP GROUND CINNAMON

1 TBSP LIGHT BROWN SUGAR

1 TBSP GRANULATED SUGAR

1 TSP GROUND GINGER

4 RUSSET POTATOES, PEELED

1 YELLOW ONION, MINCED

3 LARGE EGGS,
LIGHTLY BEATEN

¼ CUP (1½ OZ/45 G) PLUS
2 TBSP ALL-PURPOSE FLOUR

2 TBSP MINCED FRESH CHIVES

1 GARLIC CLOVE, MINCED

SALT AND FRESHLY
GROUND PEPPER

OLIVE OIL FOR FRYING

LATKES with lots of sauces

1. Preheat the oven to 200°F (95°C). Fit a baking sheet with a wire rack and set aside.

2. To make the sauces, stir together the ingredients for each in separate small bowls. Transfer to serving dishes and refrigerate.

3. Using the large holes on a box grater, shred the potatoes into a large bowl of water. Drain the potatoes and rinse under cold running water. Drain again thoroughly, squeezing to remove as much liquid as possible. Transfer the potatoes to a clean kitchen towel and squeeze to dry even further, and then place in a large bowl. Wrap the minced onion in a double thickness of paper towels, squeeze to remove as much moisture as possible, and add to the bowl. Add the eggs, flour, chives, garlic, and salt and pepper to taste and stir to mix well.

4. Pour the oil into a large frying pan to a depth of about ½ inch (12 mm) and heat over medium heat. Using your hands, scoop up a portion of the potato mixture and shape it into a ball slightly larger than a golf ball. Flatten into a very thin pancake, still blotting with paper towels as needed to remove any remaining moisture, and place in the hot oil. Repeat to add 2 or 3 more latkes to the pan, making sure not to overlap them or crowd the pan. Cook until golden brown on the first side, about 3 minutes. Using a slotted spatula, turn the latkes and cook until golden brown on the second side, 2–3 minutes longer. Transfer to the wire rack on the baking sheet and place the baking sheet in the warm oven. Repeat to cook the remaining latkes, adding them to the oven as they are finished. When all of the latkes are cooked, serve right away with the sauces.

Makin' BACON

Take it from us—curing and smoking your own bacon at home will be a great test of your improvisational skills. No matter what any recipe for curing or smoking says, you are going to end up having to get at least a little MacGyver-y to get a home-smoker setup working well. Going outside and getting your hands dirty is part of it. We suggest some beers to help ease the tension should you run into any F-bomb–inducing moments. That said, smoking bacon is about one-hundredth as stressful as assembling a crib, bike, or tree house, and you get to eat bacon at the end, so just consider it a day well spent.

The pink salt called for in the curing mix is also known as curing salt; you can find it at butcher shops, some kitchen retailers, or online. It is used in very small amounts because it contains nitrite to protect against bacteria growth, and is typically dyed pink to prevent confusing it with table salt.

WE SUGGEST some beers to EASE the tension, should you run into ANY F-bomb-inducing moments.

CURING

FOR THE CURING MIX

2 LB (1 KG) KOSHER SALT

⅔ LB (330 G) LIGHT BROWN SUGAR

¼ CUP (¾ OZ/20 G) GROUND BLACK PEPPER

¼ TSP PINK SALT (PAGE 24)

5-LB (2.5-KG) SLAB OF SKIN-OFF PORK BELLY

Important: Do not let the pink salt touch your skin. Put on a pair of disposable gloves, if you have them.

Combine all of the ingredients for the curing mix in a large bowl and stir until well blended.

Into a nonreactive container (meaning plastic, ceramic, glass, or stainless steel) large enough to hold the pork belly, sprinkle a layer of curing mix. Lay the pork belly in the container and sprinkle the remaining curing mix all over it. Use gloved hands or a spoon to rub the mix into the sides of the pork belly or anywhere the flesh is still exposed. You want the pork completely coated. Wrap tightly with plastic wrap and refrigerate for 2 days.

At the end of the second day, test the cure on your pork belly. Cut off the thinnest possible slice to expose the interior, and discard. Cut another slice ¼ inch (6 mm) thick to use as your test slice. First, evaluate the look and feel of the meat. It should be quite firm and dry looking. Next, taste it by cooking the meat in a frying pan as you would cook a slice of bacon. It should be very well seasoned and slightly sweet. If the belly isn't firm, dry, and quite flavorful—well, let it go another day.

When the belly is fully cured (2–5 days), rinse it well under cold running water. Pat it dry and place it on a wire rack or plate lined with paper towels. Refrigerate overnight to make sure it's good and dry. Now you're ready to smoke.

SMOKING

The most important thing to keep in mind when home-smoking is this: Do not let your fire get too hot. You want to draw out the smoking process for at least 2 hours, and if the fire is too hot, you'll overcook your bacon before it absorbs the smoke. You'll need a charcoal grill and an instant-read meat thermometer.

Soak 1 lb (500 g/4–5 cups) applewood chips in water to cover for an hour before you begin. Scrape the grill rack and oil it. Fire up a medium-sized pile of charcoal in one corner of the grill. Let the flames die down and place the pork belly on the rack far from the fire. Sprinkle a handful of drained wood chips on top of the hot coals. Cover the grill and allow a smoke to build. Check for smoke by opening the vent. You should see anything from a few wisps to a full-on smoke attack. (Close the vent after checking.)

Now, let the smoke do its thing. Check the vent every 20 minutes. Add some more coals if needed to build the fire back up, and keep adding wood chips to maintain a solid cloud of smoke. Don't let the heat go above 250°F (120°C) in the grill (closer to 150°F/65°C is ideal) and don't let the internal temperature of the pork belly get higher than 155°F (68°C).

After 2 hours, take your pork belly off the fire. It should be beautifully caramelized with the fat just barely melted, but not fully cooked. It should have a nice, thick, smoky aroma. It should be . . . bacon.

Let the bacon cool in the fridge, then slice it lengthwise into ¼-inch (6-mm) slices and then wrap in plastic wrap until ready to use. It'll keep in the fridge for 2 weeks or freeze beautifully. Cook it just like any bacon, in a frying pan or in the oven. Now clear your schedule and stuff your face with bacon.

POLENTA IS CRAZY VERSATILE. IT WORKS WELL WITH LOTS OF DIFFERENT FLAVORS AND TEXTURES. YOU MIGHT EXPECT TO FIND GRITS IN A BRUNCH CHAPTER, AND GO AHEAD AND USE THEM IF YOU CAN'T FIND GOOD POLENTA. BUT WHEN YOU SWIPE PERFECTLY SAUTÉED ASPARAGUS THROUGH WARM RUNNY EGG YOLKS AND CHEESY POLENTA, YOU'LL FORGET ABOUT ANY BREAKFAST GRITS YOU'VE EVER HAD.

SERVES 4

cheesy polenta with POACHED EGGS

and SAUTÉED ASPARAGUS

FOR THE POLENTA

1 CUP (7 OZ/220 G) POLENTA

1 CUP (8 FL OZ/250 ML) HEAVY CREAM

2 TBSP UNSALTED BUTTER

¼ CUP (1 OZ/30 G) FRESHLY GRATED PARMESAN CHEESE

SALT

2 TBSP EXTRA-VIRGIN OLIVE OIL

1 BUNCH ASPARAGUS, TRIMMED AND SPLIT LENGTHWISE

FRESHLY GROUND PEPPER

8 LARGE EGGS, AT ROOM TEMPERATURE

1. To make the polenta, in a large saucepan over low heat, combine the polenta and 3 cups (24 fl oz/750 ml) water and slowly bring to a simmer. Cook, stirring often, until the polenta has thickened and the grains are almost tender, about 30 minutes or according to package directions. Add the cream, butter, and Parmesan and cook, stirring constantly, until the mixture thickens and pulls away from the sides of the pan. Season with salt to taste. Set aside and cover to keep warm.

2. In a large frying pan, heat the olive oil over high heat until it begins to smoke. Add the asparagus to the pan, sprinkle with salt and pepper to taste, and toss quickly to coat. Cook, tossing a few more times, until the asparagus is nicely browned and just tender, 2–3 minutes. Transfer to paper towels to drain.

3. In a large sauté pan, bring a generous amount of water to boil. Reduce the heat to maintain a gentle simmer. Working with 4 eggs at a time, break each carefully into a cup and slide them into the simmering water. Cook for 3–5 minutes, depending on how runny you like your yolks. Remove from the water with a slotted spoon and blot the underside dry with paper towels. Repeat to cook the remaining 4 eggs.

4. While the eggs are poaching, spoon a generous mound of the polenta onto each of 4 plates. Carefully slide 2 eggs on top of each mound of polenta. Season with salt and pepper. Arrange the asparagus spears alongside the polenta, dividing them evenly. Serve right away.

WE WANTED TO INCLUDE A BREAKFAST DISH THAT IS A LITTLE MORE REFINED. HERE IT IS. THIS TART LOOKS AND TASTES AMAZING. YOU'LL IMPRESS PEOPLE IF YOU SERVE IT FOR BRUNCH, GUARANTEED.

ONION, Gruyère, and potato TART

SERVES 4

FOR THE TART DOUGH

1¼ CUPS (6½ OZ/200 G) ALL-PURPOSE FLOUR

SALT

1 STICK (½ CUP/4 OZ/125 G) COLD UNSALTED BUTTER, CUT INTO SMALL CUBES

2 TBSP ICE WATER, PLUS MORE IF NEEDED

4 TBSP (2 FL OZ/60 ML) OLIVE OIL

2 WHITE ONIONS, DICED

½ LB (250 G) FINGERLING POTATOES, HALVED LENGTHWISE

OLIVE OIL COOKING SPRAY

½ TSP FRESHLY GROUND PEPPER

4 TSP HEAVY CREAM

1 CUP (4 OZ/125 G) SHREDDED GRUYÈRE CHEESE

1. To make the dough, in a large bowl, whisk together the flour and ¼ tsp salt. Scatter the butter cubes on top and toss to coat with the flour mixture. Using a wooden spoon, beat until the mixture looks like coarse cornmeal. Add the 2 Tbsp ice water and mix until a rough dough forms, adding more water as needed. Form into a ball, wrap in plastic, and refrigerate for at least 3 hours or up to overnight.

2. In a frying pan, heat 2 Tbsp of the olive oil over high heat. When the oil is very hot, add the onions and sauté until browned on the edges, about 2 minutes. Reduce the heat to low and cook, stirring often, until the onions are very tender and caramelized to a deep, golden brown, about 20 minutes. Remove from the heat and set aside.

3. Meanwhile, in another frying pan, heat the remaining 2 Tbsp olive oil over medium-high heat. Add the potatoes and spread in an even layer. Cook for about 4 minutes so a nice golden crust forms, then turn with a spatula and continue to cook for about 4 minutes longer, until golden on the other side and tender. Remove from the heat and set aside.

4. Preheat the oven to 375°F (190°C). Spray a 9½-inch (24-cm) tart pan lightly with cooking spray. Remove the dough from the fridge, unwrap, and place on a floured work surface. Dust a rolling pin. Roll the dough out to a thickness of about ⅛ inch (3 mm). Place the dough in the prepared pan and press it gently but firmly into the bottom and up the sides. Prick the bottom with a fork. Bake for 10 minutes without filling. Arrange the potatoes in the bottom of the shell, then top with the onions. Drizzle with the cream and scatter the cheese over the top. Bake until the cheese is golden brown and bubbling, about 20 minutes. Let cool slightly, then serve.

Turkish baked EGGS

SERVES 3-4 →

WE COULD USE THIS SPACE TO SHARE A HISTORY LESSON ABOUT THIS DISH AND ITS CIRCASSIAN AND SYRIAN ORIGINS BUT LET'S JUST LEAVE IT AT THIS: IT'S NOT AN OMELET AND IT'S NOT A FRITTATA. IT'S JUST REALLY GOOD. ANYWAY, IF YOU WANT A HISTORY LESSON I'M SURE YOU HAVE A COMPUTER LYING AROUND SOMEWHERE. IT'S CALLED GOOGLE.

FOR THE TOMATO SAUCE

1 CAN (28 OZ/875 G) WHOLE PLUM TOMATOES, PREFERABLY SAN MARZANO, DRAINED

2 TBSP OLIVE OIL

1 GARLIC CLOVE, MINCED

1 TSP GROUND CUMIN

½ TSP GROUND CORIANDER

¼ TSP CAYENNE PEPPER (OPTIONAL)

SALT

1 TBSP OLIVE OIL

1 BAG (10 OZ/285 G) BABY SPINACH

6 LARGE EGGS

1 CUP (5 OZ/155 G) CRUMBLED FETA CHEESE

½ CUP (4 OZ/125 G) GREEK YOGURT

½ CUP (4 FL OZ/125 ML) WHOLE MILK

ZEST OF 1 LEMON

1. Preheat the oven to 375°F (190°C).

2. To make the sauce, pour the tomatoes into a bowl and break up into chunks with your hands. In a medium saucepan, heat the 2 Tbsp olive oil over medium heat. Add the garlic and toast, stirring, for about 30 seconds. Add the tomatoes, cumin, coriander, cayenne, if using, and a big pinch of salt and simmer until the sauce has reduced and thickened but does not seem too dry, 10–15 minutes. Taste and adjust the seasoning. Remove from the heat and cover to keep warm.

3. In a medium frying pan, heat the 1 Tbsp olive oil over medium-high heat. Add the spinach and quickly sauté until just wilted, 1–2 minutes, stirring in a pinch of salt toward the end. Remove from the heat and set aside.

4. Pour the tomato sauce into a 9-inch (23-cm) square glass baking dish and spread smooth. Cover evenly with the wilted spinach. Using the back of a spoon, make 6 evenly spaced indentations in the spinach, each just large enough to hold an egg. Carefully crack 1 egg into each well, taking care not to break the yolks. Sprinkle the feta over the top, distributing it evenly. Bake until the whites are just set, 20–25 minutes.

5. While the eggs are baking, whisk the yogurt and milk together in a small saucepan and warm over low heat. Whisk in the lemon zest. Remove the eggs from the oven, spoon the yogurt sauce over the top, and serve directly from the dish.

EVERY SUMMER FOR ABOUT 20 YEARS, OUR MOM'S SIDE OF THE FAMILY RENTS A HOUSE IN A DIFFERENT PART OF MICHIGAN. WE ALL COME TOGETHER TO SIT ON THE BEACH, COOK UP A STORM, AND PLAY REALLY COMPETITIVE GAMES OF SCRABBLE. THIS PAST YEAR, I MADE CINNAMON BUNS FOR BREAKFAST BUT USED AN ENTIRE JAR OF NUTELLA. WITH THAT SIMPLE ADDITION, THIS BRILLIANT RECIPE WAS BORN. —ELI

MAKES 12 BUNS

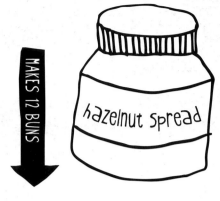

nutella BUNS

FOR THE DOUGH

1 PACKAGE (2¼ TSP) ACTIVE DRY YEAST

1 TSP GRANULATED SUGAR, PLUS ¼ CUP (2 OZ/60 G)

½ CUP (4 FL OZ/125 ML) WHOLE MILK

4 TBSP (2 OZ/60 G) UNSALTED BUTTER, AT ROOM TEMPERATURE

1 TSP KOSHER SALT

2 LARGE EGGS, BEATEN

1 TSP PURE VANILLA EXTRACT

4 CUPS (20 OZ/625 G) ALL-PURPOSE FLOUR, PLUS MORE FOR DUSTING

VEGETABLE OIL FOR BOWL

5 TBSP (2½ OZ/75 G) UNSALTED BUTTER, PLUS MORE FOR BAKING DISH

¾ CUP (6 OZ/185 G) PACKED BROWN SUGAR

⅔ CUP (3½ OZ/105 G) ROUGHLY CHOPPED PECANS

1½ CUPS (7½ OZ/235 G) NUTELLA

1 LARGE EGG, BEATEN, FOR EGG WASH

GROUND CINNAMON

1. To make the dough, pour ½ cup (4 fl oz/125 ml) warm water (110°F/43°C) into a small bowl. Add the yeast and the 1 tsp granulated sugar and stir to dissolve. Let stand until frothy, 5–10 minutes. Meanwhile, in a small saucepan, heat the milk just until it begins to bubble. Remove from the heat and stir in the ¼ cup granulated sugar, the 4 Tbsp butter, and the salt. Set aside until cool.

2. In a large bowl, stir together the yeast mixture, the milk mixture, the eggs, the vanilla, and half of the flour. Stir in the remaining flour, a little at a time. Turn the dough out onto a well-floured work surface and knead, dusting with more flour as needed, until smooth and not sticky, about 5 minutes. Place in an oiled bowl and turn to coat. Cover and let rise in a warm place until doubled in volume, about 1 hour.

3. Preheat the oven to 375°F (190°C). Melt the 5 Tbsp butter in a small saucepan over medium heat. Whisk in the brown sugar until smooth. Pour the brown sugar mixture into a greased 9-by-13-inch (23-by-33-cm) baking dish. Scatter the pecans on top.

4. On a well-floured work surface, roll the dough out into a rectangle about 15 by 20 inches (38 by 50 cm). Spread the Nutella over the dough in a thin layer, leaving a ½-inch (12-mm) border uncovered on one long side. Brush the border with the beaten egg. Starting with the covered long side, roll the dough gently into a cylinder, pressing to seal the seam with the egg. Sprinkle all over with cinnamon. Cut crosswise into 12 rounds and place in the baking dish on top of the pecans. Bake until golden brown, 20–25 minutes. Let cool slightly, then invert onto a large platter. Spread any of the brown-sugar mixture left in the dish onto the rolls and serve.

DO NOT TRY TO TEND THE FIRE, FOR THAT IS IMPOSSIBLE. ONLY TRY TO REALIZE THE TRUTH: IT'S NOT THE FIRE THAT COOKS THE FOOD, IT IS YOU.

Backyard Grub

WATERMELON GAZPACHO 34

GRILLED PEACH SALAD 37

GRILLED ROMAINE AND BACON SALAD 38

FRIED GRAPE SALAD WITH HAZELNUTS AND BLUE CHEESE 39

SUMMER PANZANELLA 40

GRILLED MEATBALL SANDWICH 43

PROJECT PICKLING 44

GRILLED FLANK STEAK WITH CHILE SPICE RUB 48

GRILLED WHOLE CHICKEN 50

GRILLED HOT WINGS 51

GRILLED WHOLE FISH 53

ROASTED SUMMER SQUASH 54

SAUTÉED GREENS WITH ALMONDS AND CURRANTS 55

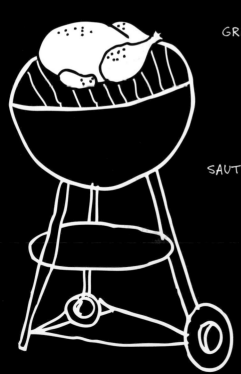

WATERMELON GAZPACHO? A GAZPACHO MADE WITH TOMATOES? HOW IS THAT EVEN POSSIBLE, YOU ASK? HOW DID THE RECIPE END UP WITH THAT TITLE? WELL, IT'S ACTUALLY PRETTY SIMPLE. WE TYPED "WATERMELON" AND THEN IMMEDIATELY TYPED "GAZPACHO." YOU'LL THANK US.

SERVES 4

WATERMELON gazpacho

I SEEDLESS WATERMELON, CUBED

½ RED ONION, CUT INTO BIG CHUNKS

½ YELLOW BELL PEPPER, SEEDED AND CUT INTO BIG CHUNKS

I CUP (4 OZ/I25 G) ALMONDS

5 THICK SLICES SOURDOUGH BREAD

½ CUP (4 FL OZ/I25 ML) EXTRA-VIRGIN OLIVE OIL, PLUS MORE FOR BRUSHING

SALT

1. Preheat the oven to 350°F (180°C).

2. In a food processor, process the watermelon to a smooth purée. Strain the juice through a medium-mesh sieve into a large bowl; you should have about 4 cups (1 qt/1 l). Add the onion and bell pepper to the food processor (no need to clean it first) and process to a smooth purée. Add to the bowl with the watermelon juice and place in the fridge. Reserve the food processor (again, no need to clean it).

3. Spread the almonds on a baking sheet. Brush 1 slice of the bread with olive oil and put it on the pan alongside the nuts. Bake until the bread is lightly golden and the nuts are fragrant and golden, about 10 minutes. Shake the tray a few times during toasting so the almonds don't scorch, and turn the bread once halfway through. Set aside to cool. Cut the bread into ¼-inch (6-mm) cubes and set aside for garnish.

4. Cut the crusts off the remaining 4 bread slices. Break the bread into large pieces, add to the food processor, and process to crumbs. Remove the watermelon mixture from the fridge and add the bread crumbs. Put the toasted almonds in the food processor and pulse to finely chop. Work carefully, as you don't want the nuts to turn to paste. Add to the watermelon mixture. Add the ½ cup olive oil and salt to taste and stir to mix well. Refrigerate until well chilled, at least 1 hour. Taste and adjust the seasoning. Ladle into soup bowls, garnish with the reserved bread cubes, and serve.

WE WERE SITTING AROUND, BULLSHITTING ABOUT DESSERT RECIPES. WE BOTH LOVE PEACHES AND WE BOTH LOVE GRILLING SO THAT SEEMED NATURAL. A FEW HOURS LATER, RADICCHIO, PROSCIUTTO, AND RICOTTA ENTERED THE DISCUSSION AND THIS SAVORY DISH WAS BORN. THAT PRETTY MUCH SUMS UP WHAT'S SO FUN ABOUT COOKING.

SERVES 4-6 →

Grilled PEACH Salad

1 TBSP UNSALTED BUTTER

½ CUP (¾OZ/20 G) PANKO BREAD CRUMBS

½ TSP DRIED HERBES DE PROVENCE

5 TBSP (3 FL OZ/80 ML) EXTRA-VIRGIN OLIVE OIL, PLUS MORE FOR GRILL

3 RIPE FREESTONE PEACHES, PITTED AND CUT INTO THICK WEDGES

1 SMALL HEAD RADICCHIO, CORED AND SEPARATED INTO LEAVES

KOSHER SALT AND FRESHLY GROUND PEPPER

2 TBSP APPLE CIDER VINEGAR

2 TBSP HONEY

½ CUP (4 OZ/125 G) RICOTTA CHEESE

8 PAPER-THIN SLICES PROSCIUTTO, TORN

1. In a frying pan over medium heat, melt the butter. Add the bread crumbs, stir to coat with the butter, and sauté until toasty and golden brown, 3–5 minutes. Stir in the herbes de Provence, then remove from the heat and set aside.

2. Build a medium-hot fire in a charcoal grill or preheat a gas grill to medium-high. Using a grill brush, scrape the heated grill rack clean. Rub the rack with oil.

3. In a bowl, combine the peaches, radicchio, 2 Tbsp of the olive oil, and ½ tsp salt and toss to coat. Turn out onto the grill rack and arrange evenly over the heat with tongs. Grill, turning as needed, until the peaches are nicely grill-marked, tender, and warmed through and the radicchio is slightly wilted, 2–4 minutes. Transfer to a plate and set aside.

4. In a large bowl, whisk together the remaining 3 Tbsp olive oil, the vinegar, the honey, and salt and pepper to taste. Add the grilled peaches and radicchio. Add the ricotta in 1-inch (2.5-cm) spoonfuls. Toss to mix well. Arrange the salad on a serving platter. Garnish with the torn prosciutto and toasted bread crumbs and serve right away.

WHEN YOU CONSIDER THAT BACON IS OFTEN THE REASON VEGETARIANS BEGIN EATING MEAT AGAIN, THE STATEMENT "EVERYTHING IS BETTER WITH BACON" IS OFFENSIVELY WEAK. THE STATEMENT SHOULD REALLY BE "BACON CAN COMPLETELY ALTER A PERSON'S PERSONAL CONVICTIONS, DIETARY RESTRICTIONS, AND RELIGIOUS BELIEFS IN ONE SINGLE BITE."

Grilled
romaine and bacon
SALAD ← SERVES 4

8 OZ (250 G) SLAB BACON, CUT CROSSWISE INTO SMALL CHUNKS

FOR THE VINAIGRETTE

2 TBSP APPLE CIDER VINEGAR

1 TSP DIJON MUSTARD

1 TBSP EXTRA-VIRGIN OLIVE OIL

SALT AND FRESHLY GROUND PEPPER

2 HEARTS OF ROMAINE LETTUCE, CORED AND SEPARATED INTO LEAVES

2 TBSP EXTRA-VIRGIN OLIVE OIL, PLUS MORE FOR GRILL

1 APPLE, PREFERABLY GRANNY SMITH OR HONEYCRISP, CORED AND SLICED

¼ CUP (1 OZ/30 G) TOASTED PUMPKIN SEEDS

1. In a frying pan over medium-low heat, cook the bacon until crisp, about 5 minutes. Transfer to paper towels to drain. Reserve the bacon fat for the vinaigrette.

2. To make the vinaigrette, in a bowl, whisk together the vinegar, mustard, the 1 Tbsp olive oil, 2 Tbsp of the warm bacon fat, and salt and pepper to taste. Add a little more bacon fat if you like a smokier flavor.

3. Build a hot fire in a charcoal grill or preheat a gas grill to high. Using a grill brush, scrape the heated grill rack clean. Rub the rack with oil. In a large bowl, combine the romaine leaves with the 2 Tbsp olive oil and a pinch of salt and toss to coat thoroughly. Working in batches if necessary, arrange the leaves in a single layer on the grill rack and grill until just wilted, turning once, 2–3 minutes.

4. As it comes off the grill, transfer the wilted romaine to a large salad bowl. Add the vinaigrette, bacon, and apple and toss well. Taste and adjust the seasoning. Garnish with the pumpkin seeds and serve right away.

MOST PEOPLE HAVEN'T EATEN FRIED GRAPES
BEFORE, SO DON'T BE SURPRISED WHEN THE
REACTIONS TO THIS SALAD MAKE IT SEEM LIKE
YOU'VE JUST UNVEILED A HOMEMADE TURDUCKEN.
BUT LET'S NOT SELL YOUR ABILITY OR THE
RECIPE SHORT BECAUSE THERE'S SOME
SKILL NEEDED TO MAKE THIS UNIQUE AND
TASTY SALAD. SO DON'T BUNGLE IT.

 **SERVES 4-6**

fried GRAPE SALAD
with Hazelnuts and Blue cheese

FOR THE VINAIGRETTE

4 TBSP (2 FL OZ/60 ML)
WHITE WINE VINEGAR

2 TBSP EXTRA-VIRGIN
OLIVE OIL

2 TSP HONEY

SALT

1 CUP (5 OZ/155 G)
HAZELNUTS

2 TBSP UNSALTED BUTTER

2 CUPS (12 OZ/375 G)
GREEN GRAPES

1 LB (500 G) ARUGULA OR
OTHER BITTER GREENS

1 CUP (5 OZ/155 G)
CRUMBLED BLUE CHEESE

1. To make the vinaigrette, in a small bowl, whisk together the vinegar, oil, honey, and a pinch of salt until well blended. Set aside.

2. Put the hazelnuts in a dry frying pan over medium heat. Cook, stirring constantly, until fragrant and turning lightly golden under the skins, about 5 minutes. Immediately pour onto a clean kitchen towel (the nuts can burn easily). Gather up the warm nuts in the towel and rub together to knock off the skins (you don't need to get every bit). Chop the nuts roughly and set aside.

3. In a large frying pan over medium-high heat, melt the butter and cook, stirring, until it takes on a little golden color. Add the grapes and sauté until lightly blistered and colored, 2–3 minutes. Remove from the heat and let cool, then cut each grape in half lengthwise.

4. In a large bowl, toss together the greens and vinaigrette until just combined. Add the blue cheese, hazelnuts, and grape halves and toss briefly to distribute the ingredients, taking care not to bruise the greens. Divide among individual plates and garnish with the grape bits, nuts, and cheese left in the bowl. Serve right away.

I TAKE CROUTONS SERIOUSLY. HERE, INSTEAD OF SOAKING THE
CROUTONS AND RUNNING THE RISK OF GETTING THEM SOGGY, I TOSS
THEM BRIEFLY IN THE VINAIGRETTE. THE ADDITION OF MOZZARELLA
TAKES A CUE FROM ANOTHER SIMPLE CLASSIC SALAD, THE CAPRESE,
AND BRINGS THIS TO A WHOLE NEW TASTE LEVEL. THIS IS A BREAD
SALAD...SO BUY REALLY HIGH-QUALITY BREAD. —MAX

SERVES 4 ➡

SUMMER Panzanella

**3 HEIRLOOM OR
6 PLUM TOMATOES,
RIPE BUT FIRM,
CORED AND CUT INTO
BIG CHUNKS**

**2 GARLIC CLOVES,
1 MINCED AND 1 CRUSHED
BUT LEFT WHOLE**

**2 TBSP
SHERRY VINEGAR**

2 TBSP BALSAMIC VINEGAR

**1 TBSP
EXTRA-VIRGIN OLIVE OIL,
PLUS ¼ CUP (2 FL OZ/60 ML),
PLUS MORE FOR DRIZZLING**

**½ CUP (½ OZ/15 G) PACKED
FRESH BASIL LEAVES,
PLUS MORE FOR GARNISH**

**SALT AND FRESHLY
GROUND PEPPER**

**1 LOAF CRUSTY
SOURDOUGH BREAD,
UNSLICED**

**1 BALL FRESH
MOZZARELLA DI BUFALA OR
COW'S MILK MOZZARELLA**

1. Preheat the oven to 400°F (200°C).

2. Put the tomatoes in a large bowl and add the minced garlic,
1 Tbsp of the sherry vinegar, 1 Tbsp of the balsamic vinegar,
and the 1 Tbsp olive oil. Tear the ½ cup basil leaves into the bowl
and season generously with salt and pepper. Toss to mix well. Set aside
so the flavors can develop while you make the croutons.

3. Slice the crust off the bread loaf and tear the bread into roughly 2-inch
(5-cm) pieces. Pile onto a baking sheet and toss with the ¼ cup olive oil,
a generous sprinkling of salt, and the crushed garlic. Spread in a single layer
and bake until the croutons are golden brown on the outside and still chewy
on the inside, about 12 minutes. Remove from the oven, transfer to a bowl,
and drizzle with the remaining 1 Tbsp of each of the vinegars. Toss to combine.

4. To assemble the salad, arrange the croutons and tomatoes in
a nonchalant manner on a large serving platter. Tear apart the
mozzarella and drape the pieces over the bread and tomatoes.
Garnish with a few more basil leaves and another drizzle of olive oil.
Serve right away.

SERVES 4-6 →

ALTHOUGH WE DON'T FOLLOW ANY FASHION RULES AS DICTATED BY A CALENDAR, THIS MIGHT BE AN AFTER-LABOR DAY SANDWICH BECAUSE IT CAN BE SLOPPY. IF YOU DON'T HAVE SAUCE ON YOUR FACE YOU AREN'T EATING IT RIGHT. AND IF WE HEAR A FORK OR KNIFE CLANKING ON THE PLATE, THERE WILL BE HELL TO PAY. —ELI

grilled meatball sandwich

2 LB (1 KG) GROUND BEEF

½ CUP (4 OZ/125 G) RICOTTA CHEESE

¼ CUP (1 OZ/30 G) FRESHLY GRATED PARMESAN CHEESE

¼ CUP (⅓ OZ/10 G) PANKO BREAD CRUMBS

4 LARGE EGGS, LIGHTLY BEATEN

2 TBSP MINCED FRESH FLAT-LEAF PARSLEY

1 GARLIC CLOVE, MINCED

1 TSP RED PEPPER FLAKES

KOSHER SALT

OIL FOR GRILL

1 LARGE BAGUETTE

8 OZ (250 G) THINLY SLICED PROVOLONE CHEESE

ARUGULA PESTO (PAGE 154)

1. In a large bowl, combine the beef, ricotta, Parmesan, bread crumbs, eggs, parsley, garlic, red pepper flakes, and 2 tsp salt. Mix gently just until combined; you don't want to overwork the meat. Form the mixture into 12 meatballs about the size of golf balls, putting them on a lightly oiled baking sheet as you work. Set aside at room temperature.

2. Build a hot fire in a charcoal grill or preheat a gas grill to high. Using a grill brush, scrape the heated grill rack clean. Rub the rack with oil. Arrange the meatballs on the grill rack without crowding. Using tongs, grill until browned evenly on all sides and cooked to medium, 8–10 minutes total, depending on grill temperature. Move any meatballs to a cooler area of the grill if they threaten to overbrown. Transfer to a platter or clean baking sheet as they are finished. Let rest for 5 minutes while you assemble the sandwiches.

3. Cut the baguette crosswise into fourths and split each piece horizontally. Lay the pieces, cut side down, on the grill. Toast until golden brown, about 3 minutes. Lay the provolone slices on half of the baguette pieces. Place 3 meatballs on top of the cheese-lined baguette slices. Garnish with the pesto and serve right away.

project PICKLING

Pickling is the oldest and simplest way to preserve food. Meat, fish, vegetables, and even fruits are all fair game for pickling. Vinegar, spices, and other ingredients are typically added to alter or enhance the flavor of pickled things, but salt is the real key. Here, we'll condense the entire book *Salt: A World History* into one statement: "Salt is the most important ingredient in the food history of the world, and so much so that it was once used as currency." (You're welcome, we just saved you from reading five hundred pages.) *

Pickled vegetables keep for a very long time. Therefore, pickling is a great technique for using up produce left over from making one of our recipes, an overabundant garden, or a CSA box. Pickled veggies are perfect snacks, make sandwiches *muy delicioso*, and add a layer of flavor to pasta or omelets. And, if you put the veggies to be pickled in those small glass jars (that every restaurant uses as drinking cups now), your pickles will look good enough to give away as gifts.

give pickled stuff as gifts INSTEAD of a lame bottle of wine.

* ACTUALLY THIS BOOK IS AMAZING AND YOU SHOULD READ IT

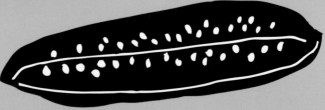

pickling LIQUID

To make your life easy, we kick off all of our pickling recipes with the exact same mixture.

2 QT (2 L) WATER

1 CUP (8 FL OZ/250 ML) WHITE VINEGAR

⅓ CUP (3 OZ/90 G) KOSHER SALT

½ CUP (4 OZ/125 G) SUGAR

1. In a large saucepan, bring the water to a boil over high heat. Stir in the vinegar. Add the salt and sugar and stir until dissolved. Remove from the heat and let cool completely.

2. Store the pickling liquid in a large plastic or glass container with a tight-sealing lid, and reach for it when you're in the pickling mood. This stuff will never go bad.

Makes about 2 qt (2 l) pickling liquid

"48 Hours" DILL PICKLES

As Nick Nolte and Eddie Murphy perfectly demonstrated, sometimes you just need two days to get it right. This pickle recipe is adapted from a super-secret 24-hour pickle recipe our cousin unlocked from his family's pickle-recipe vault (our aunt takes pickles very seriously). We thought the pickles benefited from another day, to pack more flavor in; but in a pinch, you can snack on them after Day One.

You can make as many or as few pickles as you like or want or need, using this formula. Basically settle on your number of cucumbers and make sure to cover them with pickling liquid. Don't worry if you run out of pickling liquid; it takes only a few minutes to make more.

KIRBY OR PERSIAN CUCUMBERS, SCRUBBED

GARLIC CLOVES, PEELED BUT LEFT WHOLE

LARGE FRESH DILL SPRIGS

DILL SEED (OPTIONAL)

PICKLING LIQUID AS NEEDED

1. Quarter each cucumber lengthwise. Put the cuke spears in 1-qt (32–fl oz/1-l) canning jars or other containers with tight-fitting lids. Pack them in snugly, but do not cram them in too hard, or you'll wind up with broken pickles.

2. Tuck 4 garlic cloves and 3 dill sprigs into each jar. Add ¼ tsp dill seed to each jar, if using.

3. Pour in pickling liquid to cover (leave a little space at the top). Screw the lids on tightly and place in the back of the refrigerator. Let pickle for at least 1 day but ideally 2 days, then serve or snack on them. The pickles will keep, tightly covered, in the fridge for several months.

6 lb (3 kg) cucumbers will yield about six 1-qt (32–fl oz/1-l) jars

Pickled yellow WAX BEANS

At a party with no hot girls, no booze, no good music, and no electricity, these pickled yellow beans will be a star. Note that these need a minimum of one full week to pickle. Taste them after that; add a pinch or more red pepper flakes if you want more spice.

YELLOW WAX BEANS, RINSED THOROUGHLY, ENDS TRIMMED

GARLIC CLOVES, PEELED BUT LEFT WHOLE

CORIANDER SEED

WHOLE BLACK PEPPERCORNS

RED PEPPER FLAKES

PICKLING LIQUID (PAGE 45) AS NEEDED

1. Put the beans in the desired size canning jars. Pack them in snugly, but do not cram them in too hard, or you'll wind up with broken pickled beans.

2. Tuck 4 garlic cloves into each jar (no harm in adding a couple extra cloves if using large jars). Add ¼ tsp coriander seeds, 4 black peppercorns, and a pinch of red pepper flakes to each jar.

3. Pour in pickling liquid to cover (leave a little space at the top). Screw the lids on tightly and place in the back of the refrigerator. Let pickle for at least 1 week, then serve or snack on them. The pickles will keep, tightly covered in the fridge, for several months.

4 lb (2 kg) waxed beans will yield about twelve ½-pint (8-oz/250-g) jars

pickled RAMPS

Ramps is the name for wild leeks, the first green edible thing to come up in spring in many parts of the United States. Underground lie their slender white bulbs; they look and taste like garlicky green onions or baby leeks. You can go out and forage for them yourself, or find them in the farmers' market in early spring.

You can use the tender parts of the ramp tops in omelets and other dishes that call for green onions, but only the white bulb will be good to pickle. To clean, trim the leaves off where the pink part of the stem ends and slide off the slippery outer skin of the bulb. Pickled ramps retain their crunch, but the smaller and younger the ramp, the more tender the pickle will be.

1 LB (500 G) RAMPS, LEAVES REMOVED, BULBS CLEANED AND CUT INTO ½-INCH (12-MM) PIECES (SEE NOTE AT LEFT)

GARLIC CLOVES, PEELED BUT LEFT WHOLE

PICKLING LIQUID (PAGE 45) AS NEEDED

1. Pack the ramp bulbs snugly into the desired size canning jars. Tuck 4 garlic cloves into each jar.

2. Pour in pickling liquid to cover (leave a little space at the top). Screw the lids on tightly and place in the back of the refrigerator. Let pickle for at least 1 week, then serve or snack on them. The pickles will keep, tightly covered, in the fridge for several months.

1 lb (500 g) ramps will yield about four ½-pint (8-oz/250-g) jars

PICKLED beets

Beets are pretty miraculous. We love them juiced, in salads, and roasted as a side dish. They also make gorgeous, meaty pickles. So anytime you're planning to cook with beets, consider buying a few extra and pulling out this easy recipe.

3 BEETS, ENDS TRIMMED

2 TBSP OLIVE OIL

SALT AND FRESHLY GROUND PEPPER

PICKLING LIQUID (PAGE 45) AS NEEDED

1. Preheat the oven to 375°F (190°C).

2. Place the beets in a small glass baking dish and toss with the olive oil, and salt and pepper to taste. Sprinkle 2 Tbsp water around the bottom of the dish. Cover the dish with foil and roast the beets until tender when pierced with a sharp knife, about 45 minutes.

3. Let the beets cool, then remove the skins; they should slip off pretty easily. Use a paring knife or a kitchen towel to loosen them, if needed. (We suggest wearing gloves while working with cooked beets, or your hands will get vividly and stubbornly stained.)

4. Cut each beet in half and lay it, cut side down, on a cutting board. Cut the beets into ¼-inch (6-mm) strips. Pack the beets snugly into the desired size canning jars. Pour in pickling liquid to cover (leave a little space at the top). Screw the lids on tightly and place in the back of the refrigerator. Let pickle for at least 1 week, then serve or snack on them. The pickles will keep, tightly covered in the fridge, for several months.

Three beets will yield about eight ½-pint (8-oz/250-g) jars

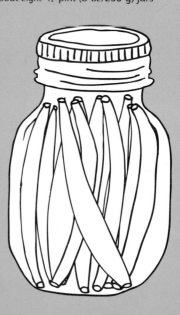

Grilled Flank STEAK WITH CHILE SPICE RUB

TAKE A PIECE OF MEAT, SEASON IT WELL, AND PUT IT ON THE GRILL. TURN IT OVER A FEW TIMES. DON'T OVERCOOK IT. THEN LET IT REST BEFORE SLICING IT AGAINST THE GRAIN. IF YOU CAN MASTER THIS BASIC TECHNIQUE AND FOLLOW THE STEPS BELOW, YOU ARE GOING TO BE ABLE TO COOK A STEAK WAY BETTER THAN ANY OF YOUR FRIENDS. —MAX

FOR THE SPICE RUB

2 TBSP KOSHER SALT

2 TSP GROUND CUMIN

2 TSP GROUND CORIANDER

1 TSP PAPRIKA

1 TSP FRESHLY GROUND BLACK PEPPER

1 TSP GARLIC POWDER

1 TSP CAYENNE PEPPER

1 FLANK STEAK, ABOUT 3 LB (1.5 KG)

OIL FOR GRILL

1. In a baking dish large enough to fit the steak, stir together all the ingredients for the spice rub. Add the steak and turn to coat thoroughly with the rub, pressing with your fingers to help it adhere to the meat as needed. Cover and let marinate in the fridge for at least 1 hour and up to 6 hours. When you are ready to cook, let the steak come to room temperature while the grill is heating.

2. Build a hot fire in a charcoal grill or preheat a gas grill to high. Using a grill brush, scrape the heated grill rack clean. Rub the grill rack with oil.

3. Place the flank steak directly over a hot area of the grill and let it sit for about 3 minutes. Rotate the steak 90 degrees, and again don't move it for another few minutes. Turn the steak and repeat the process to grill the second side: 3 minutes without disturbing, rotate, 3 more minutes. An instant-read thermometer inserted into the thickest part will read 130°F (54°C) for medium-rare. Finish cooking on a cooler part of the grill if you like your steak medium.

4. Cover the steak loosely with foil and let rest for 10 minutes. Carve it against the grain into slices about ½ inch (12 mm) thick and serve.

THE FLAVOR YOU GET FROM GRILLING A CHICKEN IS WAY MORE TASTY THAN FROM OVEN ROASTING, SO WHEN YOU'VE GOT THE TIME, THIS IS THE WAY TO DO IT. KEEP MOVING YOUR BIRD TO PREVENT FLARE-UPS FROM THE FAT DRIPPINGS ON THE COALS.

grilled whole
CHICKEN

SERVES 4

FOR THE BRINE

1 CUP (8 OZ/250 G) KOSHER SALT

¼ CUP (2 OZ/60 G) PACKED BROWN SUGAR

2 BAY LEAVES

1 TBSP WHOLE PEPPERCORNS

2 FRESH THYME SPRIGS

2 FRESH ROSEMARY SPRIGS

2 QT (2 L) ICE

1 WHOLE CHICKEN, 3–4 LB (1.5–2 KG)

1 TBSP DRIED THYME

1 TBSP DRIED ROSEMARY

OIL FOR GRILL

1. To make the brine, in a saucepan, bring 2 qt (2 l) water to a boil over high heat. Add the salt and brown sugar and stir until dissolved. Stir in the bay leaves, peppercorns, and herb sprigs and remove from the heat.

2. Put the ice in a stockpot or other container large enough to fit the brine plus the whole chicken. Pour the hot brine over the ice and refrigerate until the brine has cooled completely, about 4 hours. Add the chicken to the pot and weight it down with plates or heavy canned goods. Add cold water just as needed to make sure the bird is completely submerged in the brine. Return it to the fridge and let soak for at least 24 hours and up to 48 hours.

3. Remove the chicken from the brine and pat dry with paper towels. Using poultry shears, cut along both sides of the backbone. Press the chicken to crack the breastbone so that it lies flat. Sprinkle both sides with the dried herbs and salt. Set aside at room temperature.

4. Build a medium-hot fire in a charcoal grill or preheat a gas grill to medium-high. Scrape the heated grill rack clean and rub with oil. Place the chicken, skin side down, over a hot part of the grill and cook until well colored, 3–5 minutes. Move the chicken to a cooler area and continue cooking until the skin is golden and crispy, about 5 minutes longer. Turn and continue cooking until the chicken is opaque throughout or until an instant-read thermometer inserted into the thickest part of a thigh away from the bone registers 160°F (71°C), about 10 minutes longer. Transfer to a cutting board, tent with aluminum foil, and let rest for 5 minutes, then carve and serve.

HERE'S OUR RIFF ON BUFFALO WINGS.
THEY ARE SPICY, SWEET, AND SALTY ALL
AT THE SAME TIME. THEY WILL BE THE
BEST HOT WINGS YOU'VE EVER TASTED.
(P.S. WE CAN'T TRUST PEOPLE WHO
DO NOT LOVE HOT WINGS.)

grilled HOT WINGS

SERVES 4-6

I CUP (8 FL OZ/250 ML)
HOT-PEPPER SAUCE
(WE LIKE FRANK'S REDHOT)

I CUP (8 FL OZ/250 ML)
SRIRACHA SAUCE

ZEST AND JUICE OF 2 LIMES

FRESHLY GROUND
BLACK PEPPER

3 LB (1.5 KG) CHICKEN WINGS

OIL FOR GRILL

1. In a large bowl or zippered plastic bag, stir together the hot-pepper sauce, Sriracha, lime zest and juice, and 1 tsp black pepper. Add the chicken wings and stir and toss to coat thoroughly, or zip the bag and turn and press to coat. Cover or seal the bag and let marinate in the fridge, stirring or turning the bag once or twice, for at least 4 hours and up to 24 hours.

2. Build a hot fire in a charcoal grill or preheat a gas grill to high. Using a grill brush, scrape the heated grill rack clean. Rub the grill rack with oil.

3. Remove the chicken wings from the marinade and discard the marinade. Arrange the wings on the grill rack and grill, turning every few minutes for even color, until opaque throughout, 10–15 minutes. Serve right away.

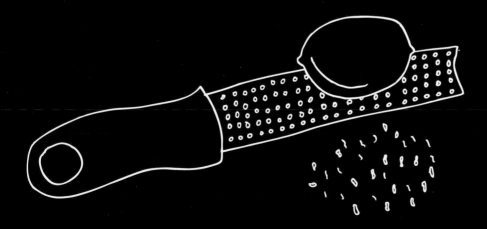

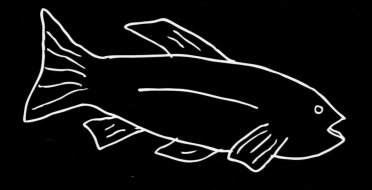

MAKE SURE YOUR GRILL SURFACE IS VERY CLEAN AND HOT BEFORE YOU PUT THE FISH ON THERE TO HELP AVOID STICKING. IF YOU TEAR THE SKIN, NO WORRIES—YOU ALWAYS HAVE ANOTHER CHANCE ON THE SECOND SIDE FOR THE FACEBOOK OR TWITTER MONEY SHOT.

grilled
WHOLE FISH

SERVES 4-6 →

I VERY FRESH WHOLE FISH, SUCH AS BRANZINO, SNAPPER, OR TROUT, ABOUT 3 LB (1.5 KG), CLEANED

2 FRESH DILL SPRIGS

3 LEMON SLICES, PLUS LEMON WEDGES FOR SERVING

SALT AND FRESHLY GROUND PEPPER

1 TBSP OLIVE OIL, PLUS MORE FOR GRILL

1. Build a hot fire in a charcoal grill or preheat a gas grill to 400°F (200°C). If using charcoal, let burn until all the coals are gray on the outside, 20–25 minutes.

2. While the grill is heating, prepare the fish: Place the dill sprigs and lemon slices inside the body cavity and sprinkle the cavity with salt. Rub the outside of the fish all over with the 1 Tbsp olive oil and sprinkle with salt.

3. Using a grill brush, scrape the heated grill rack clean. Rub the grill rack with oil. Place the fish on the grill rack over a medium-hot spot. Do not move the fish for about 5 minutes; this will help prevent the skin from sticking. Using tongs and a spatula or 2 spatulas, carefully flip the fish over and cook until the skin is crisp on the second side, 3–5 minutes longer. Use a cake tester or metal skewer to probe the temperature of the fish. If the tester doesn't feel hot, move the fish to a cooler spot on the grill, cover, and cook for another 5 minutes. The goal is to get the interior of the fish cooked and bring the skin to crispiness at the same time.

4. Transfer to a platter, garnish with the lemon wedges, and serve right away.

SUMMER SQUASH BRINGS TO MIND A TRIP ON MY BIKE TO THE FARMERS' MARKET. IT'S AN AWESOME EXAMPLE OF HOW FLAVORFUL JUST-PICKED VEGETABLES CAN BE. DON'T TAKE THIS DISH OUT OF THE OVEN TOO EARLY—THE CHEESE THAT GETS DARK AND CRISPY IS THE BEST. —MAX

ROASTED Summer Squash

SERVES 4

2 LB (1 KG) YELLOW ZUCCHINI, TRIMMED AND CUT INTO ROUNDS 1 INCH (2.5 CM) THICK

¼ CUP (2 FL OZ/60 ML) EXTRA-VIRGIN OLIVE OIL

SALT

1 TSP RED PEPPER FLAKES

2 TSP DRIED OREGANO

1 CUP (4 OZ/125 G) FRESHLY GRATED PARMESAN CHEESE

1. Preheat the oven to 425°F (220°C).

2. In a large bowl, combine the zucchini, olive oil, and salt to taste and toss to mix and coat well. Transfer to a baking sheet and spread in a single layer (use 2 baking sheets if necessary). Roast until the zucchini is a deep golden brown around the edges, 10–12 minutes.

3. Remove from the oven and, using a spatula, push the zucchini rounds as close together as possible while still leaving them in a single layer (consolidate to 1 sheet pan, if you used two). Sprinkle evenly with the red pepper flakes and oregano, and then sprinkle the Parmesan over the top.

4. Return to the oven and bake until the cheese is golden brown and bubbling, about 10 minutes longer. Remove from the oven and let cool slightly. Use the spatula to break apart the cheesy squash into large pieces and serve right away.

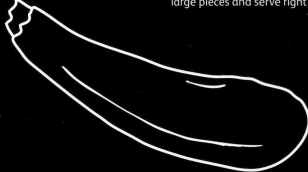

SAUTÉED GREENS ARE LIKE THE DUDE'S RUG: THEY REALLY TIE A MEAL TOGETHER. GREENS ARE ONE OF THOSE RARE THINGS THAT ARE BOTH HEALTHY AND ACTUALLY DELICIOUS. FEEL FREE TO SWITCH OUT THE KALE FOR ANOTHER STURDY GREEN LIKE SWISS CHARD IF YOU'D PREFER.

SERVES 4

SAUTÉED GREENS
with almonds and currants

½ CUP (2 OZ/60 G) MARCONA ALMONDS

I LARGE BUNCH KALE

2 TBSP EXTRA-VIRGIN OLIVE OIL

SALT

2 TBSP WHITE BALSAMIC VINEGAR

¼ CUP (1½ OZ/45 G) DRIED CURRANTS

ZEST OF I LEMON

1. If the almonds are not already toasted, put them in a dry frying pan over medium heat. Cook, stirring constantly, until fragrant and lightly golden, about 5 minutes. Immediately pour onto a plate to cool; nuts can burn easily. Chop roughly and set aside.

2. Tear each kale leaf into 4 or 5 pieces, removing the thick spine as you go. Discard the spines.

3. In a large frying pan, heat the olive oil over medium heat. Add the kale and a big pinch or 2 of salt. Cook until the kale is just tender, about 5 minutes, adding 1–2 Tbsp water as needed to keep the kale from drying out. Remove from the heat and stir in the vinegar.

4. Transfer to a serving bowl or individual plates and garnish with the currants, almonds, and lemon zest. Serve right away.

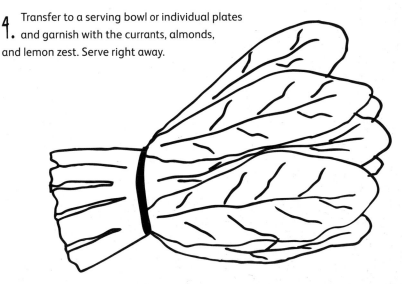

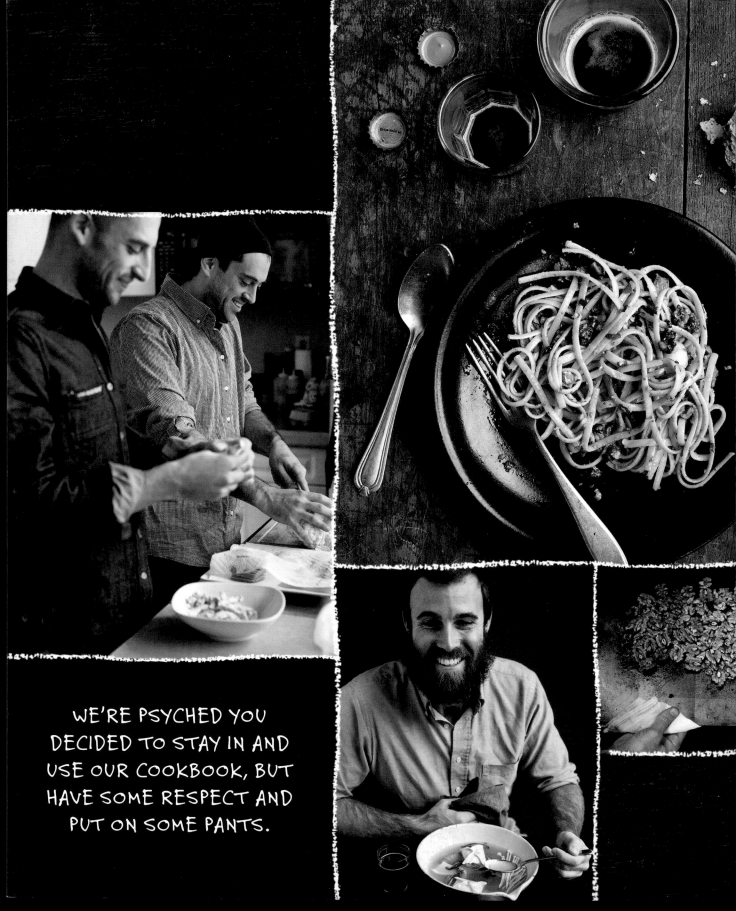

WE'RE PSYCHED YOU
DECIDED TO STAY IN AND
USE OUR COOKBOOK, BUT
HAVE SOME RESPECT AND
PUT ON SOME PANTS.

Night In

BEET AND YOGURT SALAD 58

CHICKEN ADOBO 60

WILD MUSHROOM AND ROSEMARY POTATOES 61

FORGET THE FROZEN PIZZA PROJECT 62

KOREAN-STYLE SHORT RIBS 66

SHIITAKE GINGER SOUP WITH GARLIC CHICKEN DUMPLINGS 68

BUTTER-POACHED COD WITH HERB SALAD 69

LINGUINE WITH ANCHOVIES, PARSLEY, AND WALNUTS 70

FRESH GARGANELLI WITH TOMATO, PORCINI, GUANCIALE, AND PECORINO 73

PERFECT PASTA PROJECT 74

RIGATONI WITH MEAT RAGÙ 80

PULLED PORK 81

ROASTED CAULIFLOWER WITH CARAMELIZED ONIONS 83

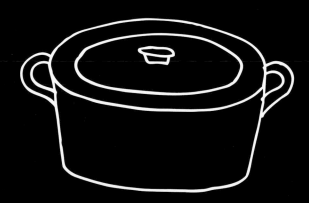

beet AND YOGURT SALAD

SERVES 4

2 LB (1 KG) BEETS, TOPS TRIMMED

2 TBSP EXTRA-VIRGIN OLIVE OIL

KOSHER SALT AND FRESHLY GROUND PEPPER

2 LEMONS

1 CUP (8 OZ/250 G) GREEK YOGURT

¼ CUP (¼ OZ/7 G) MINCED FRESH DILL

1. Preheat the oven to 350°F (180°C).

2. In a bowl, toss the beets with the olive oil and 1 tsp salt. Arrange the beets in a glass baking dish and pour in ¼ cup (2 fl oz/60 ml) water. Cover the dish tightly with foil. Roast until the beets are tender, about 1 hour. Test for tenderness by poking with a sharp knife or fork; if the blade or tines slide through easily, the beets are done. Let cool for about 30 minutes, then remove the skins by rubbing with a kitchen towel or paper towels. If the skins are thick and tough, you may need to use a vegetable peeler. Cut the beets into 1- to 2-inch (2.5- to 5-cm) pieces and set aside.

3. Remove the zest from both lemons and juice one. In a salad bowl, combine the yogurt, lemon zest, lemon juice, and half of the dill and stir to blend. Season with salt and pepper to taste. Add the beets and stir to coat evenly. Garnish with the remaining dill and serve right away.

THIS DISH IS ADAPTED FROM AN ORIGINAL FAMILY RECIPE OF A CLOSE FRIEND IN LOS ANGELES WHO WAS A PARTNER IN A FILIPINO FOOD TRUCK. THE TRUCK TORE THROUGH THE STREETS INTRODUCING HUNGRY ANGELENOS TO THE MAD TASTY FLAVORS OF FILIPINO FARE. THE FOOD RECEIVED RAVE REVIEWS. NOW YOU CAN COOK A PAINFULLY EASY VERSION OF A FAVORITE DISH AT HOME.

SERVES 2

CHICKEN adobo

2 TBSP OLIVE OIL

4 BONE-IN, SKIN-ON CHICKEN THIGHS (ABOUT 2 LB/1 KG TOTAL WEIGHT)

4 GARLIC CLOVES, MINCED

⅔ CUP (5 FL OZ/160 ML) APPLE CIDER VINEGAR

⅓ CUP (3 FL OZ/80 ML) TAMARI SOY SAUCE

6 WHOLE BLACK PEPPERCORNS

2 BAY LEAVES

STEAMED WHITE RICE FOR SERVING

1. In a Dutch oven or large, heavy-bottomed sauté pan with a tight-fitting lid, warm the olive oil over medium-high heat. Add the chicken, skin side down, and cook until golden brown, about 5 minutes. Add the garlic and sauté just until lightly browned, about 1 minute. Add the vinegar, soy sauce, peppercorns, and bay leaves. Bring the liquid to a boil, then reduce the heat to low, cover, and simmer very gently for 1½ hours, stirring occasionally.

2. To serve, spoon a bed of steamed rice onto each plate. Arrange the chicken on top of each, dividing it evenly. Pour the pan sauce over the chicken and serve right away.

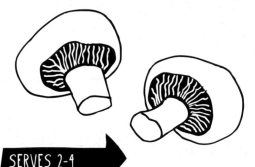

IF YOU'RE LOW ON CASH OR COOKING SKILLS, YOU MIGHT NEED SOME OF THURGOOD JENKINS' INGENUITY. SPEND THE DAY IN THE COUNTRY FORAGAING FOR WILD MUSHROOMS ("FORGET" TO PACK A PICNIC). BY THE TIME YOU GET HOME, YOUR HUNGRY DATE WILL THINK THIS TASTES LIKE A MICHELIN 3-STAR DISH.

SERVES 2-4

Wild MUSHROOM and rosemary potatoes

4 TBSP (2 FL OZ/60 ML) OLIVE OIL

½ LB (250 G) MIXED FRESH WILD MUSHROOMS, STEMMED AND ROUGHLY CHOPPED

SALT AND FRESHLY GROUND PEPPER

1 TBSP UNSALTED BUTTER

2 TBSP WHITE WINE

12 OZ (375 G) FINGERLING POTATOES, HALVED LENGTHWISE

1 TBSP MINCED FRESH ROSEMARY

1 TBSP MINCED FRESH THYME

2 GARLIC CLOVES, MINCED

¼ CUP (2 FL OZ/60 ML) HEAVY CREAM

½ LEMON

1. In a large frying pan, heat 3 Tbsp of the olive oil over high heat. When the oil is rippling (but not smoking), reduce the heat to medium and add the mushrooms. (Do not crowd the pan; add most of the mushrooms and let them shrink before you add the rest, if necessary.) Let the mushrooms cook, without stirring, for about 2 minutes.

2. Sprinkle the mushrooms with salt and pepper. Give the pan a few quick flips, tossing with your wrist, then cook, again without disturbing, for 2 minutes longer. Add the butter and let melt, then toss the mushrooms in the melted butter for about 30 seconds. Add the wine to the pan and stir and scrape to deglaze the pan. When most of the wine has evaporated, scrape the mushrooms onto a plate and set aside.

3. Return the pan to high heat. Add the remaining 1 Tbsp olive oil to the pan and let heat for about 30 seconds. Add the potatoes, rosemary, and thyme and toss quickly to coat the potatoes in the hot oil, then use tongs to arrange them cut side up. Let the potatoes cook, untouched, for 4–5 minutes. Using the tongs, turn the potatoes cut side down. Cook, again without disturbing, until the cut sides are browned, about 3 minutes longer.

4. Reduce the heat to medium, add the garlic, and toss to mix. Return the mushrooms to the pan and cook to reheat, about 30 seconds. Add the cream, quickly toss to coat the mushrooms and potatoes, and cook just until warmed through, about 15 seconds. Season with a sprinkle of salt and pepper and a squeeze or two of lemon juice and serve right away.

forget
the frozen
PIZZA

Delivery and frozen pizza are both travesties—and we don't use this term lightly. Do not look at a $10 pizza, or even a $5 pizza, as a steal. Look at it as a waste of $10. These are oversauced, flavorless pulpy circles with hardened cheese and defrosted tasteless veggies. When we see people eating frozen pizza, we knock it out of their hands and stomp on it, rendering the "pizza" inedible. (It sounds harsh, but really it's a public service.) After making this pizza recipe, you'll be baffled by why you haven't been making homemade pizza for years. Choosing from an endless choice of fresh toppings for a crust that bakes up perfectly golden brown and crispy will be a much better eating experience than shelling out some bucks for a cardboard box of cardboard crap.

In the instructions that follow, we include a dough recipe, a super-easy sauce that's fresher-tasting than anything you can buy prepared in a jar, and details for assembly, plus some classic toppings. Keep the sauce components stocked in your pantry and you will never think about frozen or soggy delivered pie again.

Do not look at a $10 pizza, OR EVEN a $5 PIZZA, as a steal. Look at it as a WASTE of $$.

PIZZA dough

1¼ CUPS (10 FL OZ/310 ML) WARM WATER (110°F/43°C)

1 PACKET (2¼ TSP) ACTIVE DRY YEAST

¼ TSP SUGAR

3 CUPS (15 OZ/470 G) ALL-PURPOSE FLOUR

2 TSP KOSHER SALT

¼ CUP (2 FL OZ/60 ML) OLIVE OIL

1. In a bowl, stir together the water, yeast, and sugar and let stand for 5 minutes. Add the flour and salt and, using a stand mixer, mix on low speed until the flour is incorporated. Add the olive oil and continue mixing until the dough is smooth and elastic, about 10 minutes.

2. Transfer the dough to a lightly oiled bowl and cover it tightly with plastic wrap. Let rise until doubled in bulk. This will take 1 or 2 hours at room temperature or, ideally, do this step ahead of time (either the morning of or the night before your pizza feed) and let the dough rise slowly in the fridge to allow more flavor to develop.

3. If your dough is refrigerated, remove it from the fridge about an hour before you're ready to bake and let it come to room temperature.

PIZZA SECRET

One of the best tricks for making a good pizza is to resist the urge to put too much stuff on it. Oversaucing, overcheesing, and overtopping will add moisture to the oven and steam the dough, making your dough soggy when you really want a nice, crispy pie. Hold back a bit and you'll have yourself a more delicious pizza.

easy pizza Sauce

1 CAN (28 OZ/875 G) WHOLE TOMATOES

2 GARLIC CLOVES, MINCED

1½ TSP KOSHER SALT

¼ CUP (2 FL OZ/60 ML) OLIVE OIL

1. Open the can of tomatoes and drain, discarding the juice. Put the tomatoes in a bowl or blender. Using an immersion blender or processing on high speed, purée the tomatoes until smooth. Add the garlic, salt, and olive oil and process until the sauce is nicely blended and emulsified.

2. If you're not using it right away to sauce up your dough, it can be stored in an airtight container in the fridge for up to 1 week.

If you want to get serious about pizza, think about investing in a baking stone and peel. Baking directly on a stone is something that makes a huge difference between a pizza from a home oven and one from a great pizzeria. Let the stone heat up in the oven for at least 30 minutes before baking on it. You'll also need a peel, which is a wooden surface with a handle. Lightly flour the peel and build the pizza directly on it. Slide the prepared pizza off the peel directly onto the stone. When the pizza's done, use the peel to remove it from the stone. Slide the pie onto a cutting board and cut away.

POTLUCK PIZZA

Instead of having friends over just to "drink socially" or to play Settlers of Catan, why not have them come over to do that and also help make dinner? Tell everyone to bring one ingredient that truly represents their individuality (fritos, fresh fruit, palak paneer, refried beans, nuts, quinoa). You're gonna have to make the dough and the sauce and grocery shopping is a bitch so this is basically a sneaky way to not pay for everything else.

Pizza like the pros

1 RECIPE PIZZA DOUGH (PAGE 63)

2 TBSP OLIVE OIL

1½ CUPS (12 FL OZ/375 ML) EASY PIZZA SAUCE (PAGE 63)

ANY TOPPINGS YOU LOVE

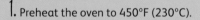

1. Preheat the oven to 450°F (230°C).

2. Make sure the dough is at room temperature before you begin. Spread the olive oil evenly on the bottom of a baking sheet. Flour your hands, then carefully take up the dough and place it on the oiled pan. While taking care to handle the dough as little as possible (this safeguards against air bubbles), push and pull and spread it to cover the pan evenly and to the edges. The dough will spring back and also slide around on the oil, so you may have to stretch it over the edges of the pan to end up with the desired size.

3. Spread the sauce evenly over the surface of the dough. Add the desired toppings. Bake until the dough crisps and the sauce starts to bubble, 5–10 minutes. Cut into wedges and serve.

FAVORITE combos

margherita

For this classic red pie, after saucing the pizza, break up about 4 oz (125 g) fresh mozzarella into 1-inch (2.5-cm) chunks and dot them evenly over the pizza. After baking, top with fresh basil leaves.

bacon & blue cheese

Cut ½ lb (250 g) bacon into small dice and cook it in a frying pan over medium-high heat until crispy. Remove from the heat and drain the fat. Sprinkle evenly over the pizza, followed by about 1 cup (5 oz/155 g) crumbled blue cheese before baking.

Italian sausage, escarole & Parmesan cheese

Cover the dough with a layer of tomato sauce, then 1 cup of torn escarole leaves. Crumble ¼ lb (125 g) of cooked Italian sausage and space evenly over the top of the pie. Sprinkle 2 Tbsp freshly grated Parmesan cheese and a drizzle of olive oil over the top before baking.

leftover specials

Sauce your pie with the spicy tomato sauce in the recipe on page 73 and finish it off with other toppings like fresh basil leaves, thinly sliced guanciale, red onion, and/or sliced garlic before baking.

Use leftovers from your pesto and meatball sandwich (page 43) to transform a pizza. Spread the pesto on the dough and dot with meatball pieces then add mozzarella cheese and dried crushed chiles before baking. Add a handful of fresh arugula on top just before serving.

capers, anchovies & parsley

Drizzle on a layer of olive oil then sprinkle 1 Tbsp drained capers over the top. Evenly space 6 anchovy fillets and a few dollops of ricotta cheese. Top with a sprinkle of red pepper flakes or diced fresh chiles for heat, if desired. When the pie is cooked, finish with 1 Tbsp chopped fresh parsley and a squeeze of lemon.

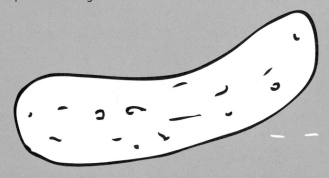

I LOVE GOING OUT FOR KOREAN BBQ. WHILE A HUGE PART
OF THE EXPERIENCE IS SAMPLING ALL OF THE NEVER-ENDING
BANCHAN THAT COME TO THE TABLE, THE MEAT IS THE KING OF
THE MEAL. HERE'S OUR TAKE ON MARINATED SHORT RIBS THAT ARE
AS FLAVORFUL AS ANYTHING WE'VE TASTED AT A RESTAURANT.
MARINATE THESE RIBS OVERNIGHT, PICK UP SOME KIMCHI ON YOUR
WAY HOME, AND YOU'VE GOT THE PERFECT KOREAN-STYLE
DATE NIGHT WITHOUT THE SMELLY CLOTHES. –ELI

Korean-style
SERVES 2-4
SHORT ribs

1 CUP (8 FL OZ/250 ML)
SOY SAUCE

¼ CUP (2 FL OZ/60 ML)
RICE VINEGAR

2 TBSP WHITE VINEGAR

⅓ CUP (2½ OZ/75 G)
TIGHTLY PACKED
DARK BROWN SUGAR

3 TBSP SRIRACHA SAUCE,
PLUS MORE FOR SERVING

1 TBSP GROUND
BLACK PEPPER

½ LARGE YELLOW ONION,
CHOPPED

1 BUNCH GREEN ONIONS,
WHITE AND TENDER GREEN
PARTS ONLY, THINLY SLICED

8-10 GARLIC CLOVES,
CHOPPED

3 LB (1.5 KG) KOREAN-STYLE
SHORT RIBS

STEAMED RICE AND
HOISIN SAUCE
FOR SERVING

1. In a large bowl, whisk together the soy sauce, 1 cup (8 fl oz/250 ml) water, the vinegars, brown sugar, Sriracha, and pepper. Add the yellow onion, green onions, and garlic and stir to blend well. Add the short ribs and turn to coat well with the marinade. Cover with plastic wrap and let marinate in the refrigerator for at least 12 hours or, preferably, 24 hours.

2. Line a large, heavy-duty baking sheet with foil. Remove the ribs from the marinade and shake off the onions and garlic. Place on the prepared baking sheet and let come to room temperature (this could take up to an hour).

3. Preheat the broiler. Broil the ribs until the surface of the meat begins to caramelize, 5–7 minutes. Remove from the broiler, turn, slide back under the broiler, and broil until cooked through, about 5 minutes longer. Remove from the broiler and serve right away with the rice, hoisin sauce, and additional Sriracha.

WHILE THERE ISN'T ANYTHING TRADITIONALLY THAI ABOUT THIS SOUP, IT REMINDS ME OF A SOUP I USED TO GET AT A LITTLE THAI PLACE ON THE PACIFIC COAST HIGHWAY. I'D SIP SOME OF THAT RESTAURANT'S AMAZING BROTH WHILE WATCHING THE OCEAN. THIS RECIPE IS IN HOMAGE TO MY MALIBU TIME. IT'S AN AWESOME SOUP. —ELI

SERVES 4-6

Shiitake GINGER SOUP with GARLIC Chicken dumplings

3 TBSP VEGETABLE OIL

1 LB (500 G) BONE-IN, SKIN-ON CHICKEN BREAST

SALT AND FRESHLY GROUND PEPPER

2 CUPS (16 FL OZ/500 ML) CHICKEN BROTH

5 GARLIC CLOVES, 4 CHOPPED AND 1 MINCED

¼ CUP (1 OZ/30 G) CHOPPED FRESH GINGER

2 OZ (60 G) SHIITAKE MUSHROOMS, STEMMED AND DICED

SHIITAKE BROTH (PAGE 154)

2 TBSP CHOPPED GREEN ONION

20 SQUARE WONTON WRAPPERS

1 LARGE EGG, BEATEN

1 CUP (5 OZ/155 G) SNOW PEAS

1 CUP (3 OZ/90 G) ENOKI MUSHROOMS

1. In a large, deep frying pan, warm the vegetable oil over high heat. Sprinkle the chicken with salt and pepper. When the oil is hot, place the chicken in the pan, skin side down. Cook, turning once, until browned on both sides, about 3 minutes per side. Reduce the heat to medium-low and add the chicken broth, chopped garlic, ginger, and shiitakes. Cover, bring to a simmer, and cook, stirring occasionally, until the chicken is tender, about 25 minutes. Remove from the heat and transfer the chicken to a plate; strain the cooking liquid, discard the solids, and return it to the pan. When cool enough to handle, pull the meat from the bones and chop finely. Return the chopped chicken to the cooking liquid, return to a simmer over low heat, and cook for 10 minutes longer. Remove from the heat and set aside to cool.

2. Put the shiitake broth in a soup pot and maintain a very low simmer. To make the dumplings, using a slotted spoon, transfer the chicken from its cooking liquid to a bowl and discard the cooking liquid. Add the green onion and minced garlic and mix well. Place a wonton wrapper on a clean work surface and, using a pastry brush dipped in the beaten egg, paint about a ½-inch (12-mm) border around all sides. Place a tsp of the chicken mixture in the center of the wrapper. Fold up all 4 corners to meet in the center and press together to seal. Repeat to fill all of the wonton wrappers. Add any extra chicken mixture to the broth.

3. Place the dumplings in the simmering broth and raise the heat to medium. After about 3 minutes, add the snow peas and enoki mushrooms and bring to a boil. As soon as the soup begins to boil, remove from the heat. The vegetables and dumplings should be tender. Ladle into individual bowls, dividing the dumplings evenly. Serve hot.

PEOPLE WHO DON'T WORK IN RESTAURANTS USUALLY
REACT WITH FEAR AND AWE WHEN THEY SEE HOW MUCH
BUTTER PROFESSIONAL COOKS USE. BUT POACHING
FISH IN BUTTER IS A TECHNIQUE YOU SHOULD ADOPT
FOR HOME USE. SO SIMPLE AND TOTALLY DELICIOUS.
THE RICHNESS IS INCOMPARABLE. —MAX

Butter-poached COD with herb salad

SERVES 2

1 LB (500 G)
SALTED BUTTER,
CUT INTO SMALL CUBES

2 COD, HADDOCK, OR OTHER
FIRM WHITE FISH FILLETS,
ABOUT 6 OZ (185 G) EACH

KOSHER SALT AND FRESHLY
GROUND PEPPER

JUICE OF 1 LEMON

2 TBSP
EXTRA-VIRGIN OLIVE OIL

½ CUP (½ OZ/15 G) CHOPPED
MIXED FRESH HERBS SUCH
AS PARSLEY, MINT, CHERVIL,
AND/OR TARRAGON

1. In a saucepan, melt the butter slowly over medium heat. When it is completely melted and almost simmering, reduce the heat to very low. Season the fillets with salt and place them in the melted butter. Poach until just barely cooked through, 10–15 minutes, depending on the thickness. Using a cake tester, probe into the thickest part of a fillet to check for doneness; the tester should emerge very warm to the touch.

2. Meanwhile, in a bowl, whisk together the lemon juice, olive oil, and salt and pepper to taste. Add the herbs and toss to coat. Let the herb salad stand for about 10 minutes so the flavors can blend. Taste and adjust the seasoning, if necessary.

3. When the fish is done, using a wide spatula, carefully transfer the fillets to paper towels to drain briefly, then arrange each on a dinner plate. Pile the herb salad on top and serve right away.

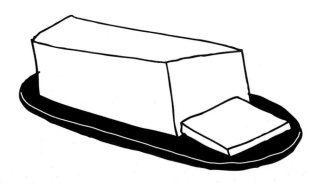

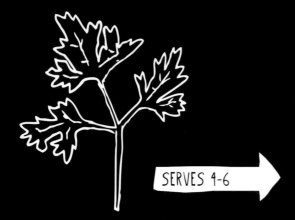

THIS IS DEFINITELY MY FAVORITE RECIPE FOR A QUICK-AND-EASY PASTA WITH A LOT OF FLAVOR. I LOVE HOW THE BRINY ANCHOVIES BALANCE OUT WITH THE RICHNESS OF THE WALNUTS AND MAKE A UNIFIED DISH. I USUALLY GO FOR AN EXTRA PINCH OF RED PEPPER FLAKES, TOO. —MAX

SERVES 4-6 →

Linguine with ANCHOVIES, parsley, and walnuts

¼ CUP (1 OZ/30 G) WALNUTS

SALT

1 LB (500 G) DRIED LINGUINE

2 TBSP
EXTRA-VIRGIN OLIVE OIL

1 GARLIC CLOVE,
CRUSHED BUT LEFT WHOLE

6 ANCHOVY FILLETS

½ TSP RED PEPPER FLAKES,
OR MORE TO TASTE

¼ CUP (¼ OZ/7 G) CHOPPED
FRESH FLAT-LEAF PARSLEY

½ LEMON

1. Put the walnuts in a dry frying pan over medium heat. Cook, stirring constantly, until fragrant and slightly darkened, about 5 minutes. Immediately pour onto a clean kitchen towel; the nuts can burn easily. Chop and set aside.

2. Bring a large pot of generously salted water to a boil over high heat. Add the pasta to the boiling water and cook until just short of al dente, or 1 minute less than the package directions for al dente.

3. While the linguine is cooking, in the frying pan over medium heat, warm the olive oil. Add the garlic clove and toast until golden brown; discard the garlic. Add the anchovy fillets, crush them into the oil with the back of a spoon, and cook until fragrant, 2–3 minutes.

4. When the linguine is ready, drain well, reserving ¼ cup (2 fl oz/60 ml) of the cooking water. Add the linguine to the frying pan along with the red pepper flakes and half of the toasted walnuts. Toss and stir over low heat until the pasta is well coated with oil and all the ingredients are evenly distributed. If the pasta appears dry, sprinkle in some of the reserved cooking water and toss again. Add the parsley and a squeeze of lemon immediately before plating. Toss one more time, divide among plates, garnish with the remaining walnuts, and serve right away.

AT ROBERTA'S, I SPENT A LOT OF TIME LEARNING HOW TO MAKE PASTA FROM SCRATCH. THIS SAUCE IS A PLAY ON AN OLD-SCHOOL, RICHLY FLAVORED ITALIAN CLASSIC CALLED AMATRICIANA. IT STICKS WELL TO THE SHAPE OF GARGANELLI. GUANCIALE IS CURED PORK JOWL, OR CHEEK MEAT. IF YOU CAN'T FIND IT, USE PANCETTA. —MAX

FRESH GARGANELLI with Tomato, Porcini, GUANCIALE, and PECORINO

◄ SERVES 4

¼ LB (125 G) GUANCIALE, DICED

½ RED ONION, FINELY CHOPPED

SALT AND FRESHLY GROUND PEPPER

2 GARLIC CLOVES, 1 CRUSHED AND 1 MINCED

2 TBSP TOMATO PASTE

1 CAN (28 OZ/875 G) WHOLE TOMATOES

½ OZ (15 G) DRIED PORCINI MUSHROOMS

1 RECIPE GARGANELLI (PAGE 78)

2 TBSP FRESHLY GRATED PECORINO CHEESE

4 FRESH BASIL LEAVES, ROUGHLY TORN

1. In a saucepan over low heat, slowly cook the guanciale until crispy, about 5 minutes. Add the onion and a pinch of salt and stir to coat the onion in the rendered fat in the pan. Raise the heat to medium and cook, stirring often, until the onion softens and caramelizes slightly, 5–10 minutes more. Add the crushed garlic clove and cook for 3 minutes longer. Add the tomato paste, stir well, and cook for another 3–4 minutes to allow the flavors to marry.

2. Pour the tomatoes into a bowl. Using your hands, break them apart into large chunks. Add the tomatoes along with their juices and the porcini mushrooms to the simmering sauce, reduce the heat to very low, and simmer gently, stirring often, until the sauce starts to thicken, 30–35 minutes. Stir in the minced garlic. Cook until nicely thickened but still saucy, about 10 minutes longer. Season with salt and pepper. Remove from the heat and cover to keep warm. (You can make the sauce ahead of time and keep it, covered tightly in the fridge, for up to 5 days.)

3. Bring a large pot of generously salted water to a boil over high heat. Add the pasta to the boiling water and cook until tender, about 3 minutes. Drain in a colander, then return to the warm pot with some of the cooking water still clinging to it. Add the warm sauce and Pecorino and toss to coat the pasta well. Fold in the basil leaves and serve right away.

perfect PASTA

Whenever you're deciding what to cook (or what to eat in general) you basically have two options: the easy way or the awesome way. The easy way is just a food placeholder till your next meal. Sure, you can buy a box of penne, cook it up, and pour some red sauce from a jar over it. You can always do that and we have done it too, a bunch of times. But making pasta and the sauce from scratch is taking that extra step to prepare something really special and completely satisfying. A plate of homemade pasta with a slow-cooked ragù is comforting and tasty in a way that doesn't even compare. For a group of friends, for that special someone, or if you just want to treat yourself to spending some time to learn a new skill—making pasta is the way to go. Then, use that skill to impress other people. Show off a little. You'll receive compliments and critical acclaim sure to enlarge your ego to dangerous proportions.

> a plate of HOMEMADE pasta with a SLOW-COOKED ragù is comforting AND TASTY IN A way that DOESN'T even compare.

Basic PASTA DOUGH

MAKES ABOUT 1½ LB (681 G); SERVES 6-8

1 CUP (5 OZ/155 G) SEMOLINA FLOUR

2 CUPS (10 OZ/315 G) ALL-PURPOSE FLOUR

4 LARGE EGG YOLKS

3 LARGE WHOLE EGGS

1. In a large bowl, mix together the flours. Make a well in the center and add the egg yolks, whole eggs, and 2 Tbsp water.

2. With a fork, whisk the eggs lightly to blend, then begin mixing all the ingredients together with your hands, drawing in flour gradually from the sides and tossing and folding until you form a cohesive ball of dough. If necessary, add another Tbsp or two of water to bring it together, but note, the finished dough will still feel somewhat dry. As long as it forms a ball, you can move to the next step.

3. Turn the dough out onto a lightly floured work surface. Knead the dough by using the heel of your hand to stretch it away from you to a thickness of about 1 inch (2.5 cm). Fold it back upon itself, push again, then rotate 90 degrees and knead a few times. Rotate 90 degrees again. Continue kneading this way for at least 10 minutes, until the dough becomes stretchy and elastic. If it springs back when you poke it, it's ready.

4. Wrap the dough in plastic wrap and let rest at room temperature for at least 1 hour and up to 12 hours before moving on to shaping.

How to use a PASTA machine

1. When your dough has rested, you're ready to roll it into pasta. Set up the machine and attach it to a clean, smooth surface. A butcher block, your dinner table, or a long counter will work fine.

2. Fill a small bowl with all-purpose flour and have it handy. Cut your ball of dough into 4 pieces to make it easier to work with, covering the pieces you're not using with a damp kitchen towel or plastic wrap.

3. Lightly flour the first piece of dough and, using your hands, press it into a flat disc about ½ inch (12 mm) thick. Set the pasta maker on the thickest setting and slowly feed in the first piece of dough. When it comes out the other side, feel the dough. It should feel soft and smooth like very firm cookie dough but not wet or sticky (if it is, dust it with flour).

4. Fold the dough onto itself and feed it through the machine again. Continue this process until the dough becomes elastic and stretchy. It will take 5–10 passes, folding each time and adding flour if necessary to prevent sticking. You'll know it's ready when you poke your finger into the dough and it bounces back slightly.

5. Now, begin thinning the dough. Take the pasta maker setting down one notch and pass the dough through it. Continue this process until the pasta is at the desired setting based on the recipe. Cover with a slightly damp kitchen towel until ready to use. Repeat with the other pieces of dough.

learn a NEW skill. Then use that skill to impress people.

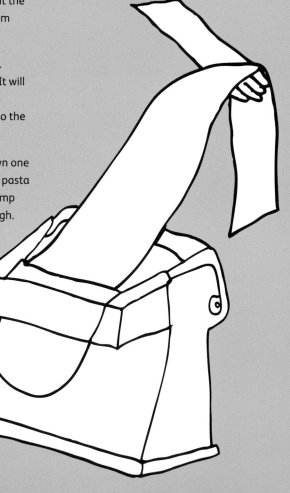

TIPS from max

When you are making pasta there are a lot of factors and variables that can seem intimidating, so we will break it down as easily as we can considering there are entire books out there dedicated to this subject.

PASTA is like pizza

I think of pasta much like pizza. Like pizza crust, if your pasta itself has great taste you're already in good shape. If you put too much stuff on a pizza it gets soggy and weird. If you put too many things in pasta the flavors get confused and it's overwhelming to eat. When you spend time making pasta by hand, highlight the pasta. Stick to about three or four main flavor components: meat, cheese, vegetable and a liquid/sauce (could be chicken/fish broth, tomato, cream, butter, or any combo).

everything I LEARNED about pasta I learned from 2 ITALIAN DUDES

While at Roberta's, I have worked with two Italian dudes who are both incredibly skilled at making pasta. Head chef Carlo Mirarchi and Angelo Romano showed me the ropes. Just hearing their names you can assume they knew way more than I did. They learned the ancient secrets of pasta from their nonnas, while my nana imparted the wisdom of putting pieces of fruit into a triple-layered jello mold.

pasta / sauce unity

Perhaps the most important thing I learned from Carlo and Angelo is that the pasta and the sauce should be one. You should not have some mystery-colored tomato liquid in your bowl when you're done eating the pasta. A lot of people have a lot to say on this subject, but I think it's pretty simple. Heavy sauce with lots of stuff in it needs big, thick noodles with body and shape. Light sauce with fewer components takes thin noodles with a lighter shape. The sauce should be thick enough to stick to the pasta. Not to get all John Nash on you, but your goal should be to create a perfect ratio of pasta to sauce in every single serving.

think about the TEXTURES

A dish is about flavor, appearance, smell, and feel. For example, a sliced piece of chicken breast on top of a pile of pasta doesn't make any sense (sorry, I know people do it all the time).

less is more This is so true on many levels and is at the foundation of how I feel about food. Just because you have the canvas doesn't mean you need to use every inch of it and every color in the paint box. The pasta should be the feature of the plate. Don't oversauce it. Let the flavor and the texture of the pasta come through. Don't overcook it. Pasta should be al dente, toothy, textured, whatever you want to call it. And make sure you boil your pasta in heavily salted water. Don't skimp on the salt in your pasta water, or everything will taste bland.

We know you're probably not going to make ravioli from scratch very often. And you know what? That's cool with us because making ravioli should be special. There are few things on earth more satisfying than a well-made ravioli. This should be one of those skills you develop and keep in your arsenal for your entire life. It's like changing a tire or building a bench. It's going to be a little tricky at first but once you make this recipe a few times, you'll be a natural.

Ravioli

Using a pasta machine, roll the dough into one long sheet that is the width of the pasta machine and is about ⅛ inch (3 mm) thick. Or, using a rolling pin, roll out the dough on a floured work surface to the same thickness. Cut the long sheet crosswise into 4 equal pieces. Place a scant tablespoon of filling evenly spaced along 1 sheet of dough, and place another sheet on top, lining up the edges. Use your fingers to press the air away from the filling, then use a ravioli press to form individual raviolis. Repeat with the remaining dough pieces. Freeze on a baking sheet lined with parchment paper until ready to use. To cook, drop into generously salted boiling water and cook for 3–5 minutes.

Garganelli

Using a pasta machine, roll the dough into sheets, stopping after you pass it through the second-thinnest setting. Let the sheets rest on a lightly floured work surface for about 10 minutes. Using a chef's knife, cut the sheets into 2-inch (5-cm) squares. Using a wooden dowel (or the handle of a wooden spoon, a pen, or any other similar rod shape) ½ inch (12 mm) in diameter, roll each square into a tube with pointed, quill-like ends. To do this, start by arranging a square in front of you with a corner pointing at you. Place the dowel horizontally on the nearest corner and press the corner gently onto the dowel to secure it. Roll the dough evenly away from you so the perpendicular corners cross the dowel at the same time and the opposite corner lines up more or less with your starting point. Squeeze gently to seal, push it off the dowel, and place on a floured baking sheet. When all of the garganelli are rolled, freeze until ready to cook. To cook, drop into generously salted boiling water and cook for 3 minutes.

This is one of my favorite shapes since it's basically a fresh version of penne, which we all know is one of the most amazing innovations of the human race alongside the printing press and Velcro. It's the same dough as the other fresh pastas, formed into a tube that holds sauce inside. It's perfectly designed for holding chunks of guanciale and red onion, so that you get a perfect bite each time. -Max

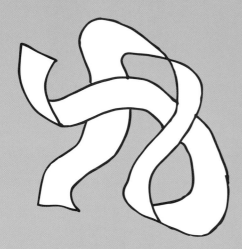

Flat egg noodles make me think of the bags of Manischewitz egg noodles that I would eat in chicken soup as a kid. Tagliatelle is the thinking man's version of egg noodles. Slightly thicker with a more interesting texture, it still goes great with a bowl of soup or just some butter and Parmesan. For this cut, the pasta should be the thickness of Patrick Bateman's business card. Make sure you test it every minute as it's cooking. The noodles should be done cooking within 3–4 minutes at the very longest. -Max

Tagliatelle

Using a pasta machine, roll the dough into sheets, stopping after you pass it through the second-thinnest setting. Let the sheets rest on a lightly floured work surface for 10–15 minutes. Using a chef's knife, cut the sheets into ribbons ¼ inch (6 mm) wide and about 10 inches (25 cm) long. Toss the strands with semolina flour to prevent sticking, wrap in plastic wrap or butcher's paper and store in the fridge for up to 1 day. To cook, drop into generously salted boiling water and cook for 3 minutes.

MORE pasta shapes

farfalle

tortellini

penne

gemelli

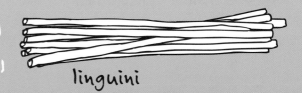
linguini

fettuccine

THERE ARE DAYS WHEN I CAN'T GET MY ACT TOGETHER TO MAKE A LAZY SUNDAY BRUNCH. SO I WAKE UP IN THE LATE AFTERNOON. CALL ELI TO SEE WHAT HE'S DOIN. "YOU THINKIN WHAT I'M THINKIN? RAGÙ! LET'S MAKE IT HAPPEN!" SLOW-COOKED PORK + BEEF + TOMATO = CRAZY DELICIOUS. —MAX

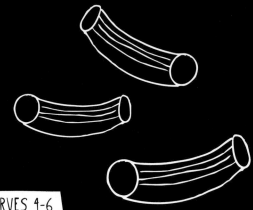

rigatoni with MEAT RAGÙ

SERVES 4-6

1 YELLOW ONION, CUT INTO 1-INCH (2.5-CM) CHUNKS

1 LARGE CARROT, PEELED AND CUT INTO 1-INCH (2.5-CM) CHUNKS

2 CELERY STALKS, CUT INTO 1-INCH (2.5-CM) CHUNKS

1 TBSP EXTRA-VIRGIN OLIVE OIL

SALT

1 LB (500 G) GROUND PORK

1 LB (500 G) GROUND BEEF

5 TBSP (3 OZ/90 G) TOMATO PASTE

1 CUP (8 FL OZ/250 ML) CHICKEN BROTH

1 LB (500 G) RIGATONI

½ TSP RED PEPPER FLAKES

¼ TSP DRIED THYME

PINCH OF GROUND CINNAMON

¼ CUP (2 FL OZ/60 ML) HEAVY CREAM

¼ CUP (1 OZ/30 G) FRESHLY GRATED PARMESAN CHEESE

1. In a food processor, combine the onion, carrot, and celery and process to a coarse purée. In a large saucepan, heat the olive oil over medium-low heat. Scrape the puréed vegetables into the pan, add a pinch of salt, and cook, stirring often, until all of the liquid cooks out and the vegetables soften, about 30 minutes. Add the pork and beef and cook, still stirring often and breaking up the meat with the spoon, until the meat is cooked through and the juices have mostly cooked out, about 45 minutes. Add the tomato paste and chicken broth and continue to cook until the sauce has reduced by half, about 5 minutes.

2. When the sauce is getting close to being done, bring a pot of generously salted water to a boil over high heat. Add the pasta and cook until al dente or according to the package directions.

3. Meanwhile, to finish the sauce, add the red pepper flakes, thyme, cinnamon, and cream and cook, stirring, until the cream thickens and the flavors have blended, about 5 minutes longer. The final consistency should be very thick but not dry. Taste and adjust the seasoning.

4. Drain the pasta, quickly add it to the ragù, and stir well to combine. Add the Parmesan and stir until the cheese is melted and the pasta and sauce are warm throughout. Serve right away.

THIS IS MY FAVORITE DISH TO MAKE FOR A BIG GROUP ON A NIGHT IN. I MADE IT ONCE FOR A SUPER BOWL PARTY AND, NOT TO BRAG, BUT IT WAS GONE BEFORE THE GAME STARTED. IT MIGHT SEEM INTIMIDATING, BUT IN REALITY YOU SLATHER SOME STUFF ON THE PORK, PUT IT IN THE OVEN, AND COME BACK EIGHT HOURS LATER FOR A MAGICAL TRANSFORMATION. IT GOES PERFECTLY WITH JALAPEÑO COLESLAW (PAGE 103). –ELI

PULLED PORK

SERVES 4-6 ➡️

2 TBSP VEGETABLE OIL

4 LB (2 KG) PORK BUTT

SALT AND FRESHLY GROUND PEPPER

1 CAN (12 FL OZ/375 ML) LAGER (WE LIKE TECATE)

1 LARGE WHITE ONION, CHOPPED

¼ CUP (2 OZ/60 G) TIGHTLY PACKED LIGHT BROWN SUGAR

1 TBSP CHILI POWDER

1. Preheat the oven to 250°F (120°C).

2. In a large Dutch oven, heat the oil over high heat. Sprinkle the pork butt generously all over with salt and pepper. Place the pork in the pot and sear, turning as needed, until a slight crust forms on all sides, about 15 minutes total.

3. Pour the beer over the pork butt. Add the onion, brown sugar, and chili powder to the pot and mix well. Cover the pot and place in the oven. Roast for 6 hours.

4. Remove the pot from the oven and use 2 forks to test the pork; it should shred easily. If it doesn't, re-cover and continue roasting until it comes apart with no resistance, up to 1 hour longer. Remove from the oven and let rest for 10 minutes, then transfer the pork butt to a cutting board or platter and shred it with your fingers, tossing out any big pieces of fat. Return to the pot and stir into the juices, then return to the oven and allow to simmer in the juices for another 1–2 hours, or until serving.

THIS HAS BEEN A GO-TO RECIPE OF MINE EVER SINCE MY DAYS OF DUMPSTER-DIVING AND VEGANISM. BACK WHEN A GOOD TAHINI SAUCE WAS A SUBSTITUTE FOR CHEESE. SOMEHOW THROUGH MY RETURN TO RAMPANT CARNIVORISM IT HAS STUCK AROUND, AS DELICIOUS AS EVER. –MAX

SERVES 4

roasted CAULIFLOWER
WITH
caramelized onions

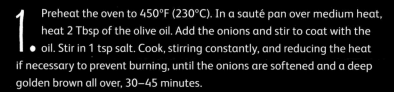

4 TBSP (3 FL OZ/90 ML) EXTRA-VIRGIN OLIVE OIL

2 YELLOW ONIONS, THINLY SLICED

SALT

½ CUP (5 OZ/155 G) TAHINI

3 TBSP FRESH LEMON JUICE

1 GARLIC CLOVE, MINCED

1 HEAD CAULIFLOWER, CUT INTO 1-INCH (2.5-CM) FLORETS

1 CUP (1 OZ/30 G) FRESH FLAT-LEAF PARSLEY LEAVES

1. Preheat the oven to 450°F (230°C). In a sauté pan over medium heat, heat 2 Tbsp of the olive oil. Add the onions and stir to coat with the oil. Stir in 1 tsp salt. Cook, stirring constantly, and reducing the heat if necessary to prevent burning, until the onions are softened and a deep golden brown all over, 30–45 minutes.

2. In a bowl, whisk together the tahini, ¾ cup (6 fl oz/180 ml) water, 1 tsp salt, the lemon juice, and the garlic and set aside.

3. Use the remaining 2 Tbsp olive oil to grease a large, heavy-duty baking sheet. Put the cauliflower florets on the pan and turn to coat well with the oil. Arrange them so they have as much space between them as possible and season with salt. Roast until nicely browned but not burned on the bottoms, about 15 minutes. Turn the cauliflower and continue to roast until browned on the second sides and tender, about 10 minutes longer.

4. Arrange the cauliflower on a platter. Garnish with the caramelized onions and parsley leaves, and drizzle with the tahini sauce. Serve right away, passing any remaining tahini sauce at the table.

A GREAT DINNER PARTY: DON'T BURN THE FOOD, NEVER RUN OUT OF BOOZE, AND MAKE SURE YOUR ITUNES DOESN'T PLAY ANY EMBARRASSING MUSIC.

Dinner Party

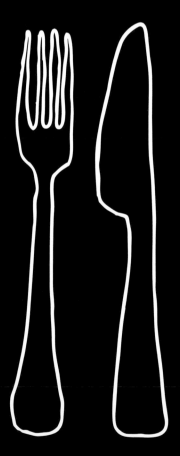

COCKTAILS PROJECT 86

medi-easternanean

AVGOLEMONO 90

ROASTED LEG OF LAMB 93   ORZO SALAD 94

GRILLED FIGS WITH BURNT HONEY AND PISTACHIO YOGURT 95

mi casa es tu taqueria

FISH TACOS WITH TOMATILLO SALSA 98

ROASTED CORN SOUP 102   JALAPEÑO COLESLAW 103

CINNAMON CHURROS 105

Sussman surf and turf

FRIED OYSTER BITES 106

PORK CHOPS WITH APPLE CHUTNEY 109

CURLY ENDIVE WITH WARM ANCHOVY VINAIGRETTE 112

ROASTED ROOT VEGETABLES WITH ROMESCO SAUCE 113

PEAR TART 114

some of Archduke franz ferdinand's favorites

CHICKEN SCHNITZEL 117

BRAISED CABBAGE WITH CARROTS AND BACON 118

CUCUMBER SALAD 119   ALMOND COOKIES 120

COCKTAILS

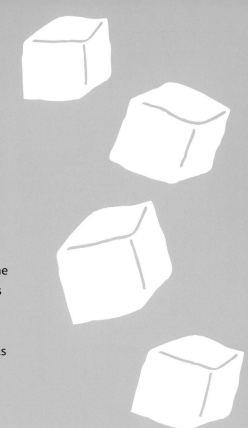

For those of you who harbor fear and intimidation about DIY mixed drinks, maybe thinking the prospect is either too fussy or too easy to fail: Serving cocktails to guests should be enjoyable and stress-free, just like drinking them. First of all, don't agonize about having a home bar that looks like a real-world bar, or go crazy stocking it. And unless you're throwing a Prohibition-style speakeasy party (which we would for sure attend but also make fun of you for having), you don't need every bar tool your favorite mustachioed, suspendered mixologist has at his disposal. Nobody at your house party wants to wait while you muddle strawberries at your kitchen counter.

Whether you're throwing a slam-bash or having a date over for a predinner drink, here are a few fast-and-easy cocktails for your new drinking and drink-making repertoire. You need fewer than ten basic items for a sick bar setup: a shaker, bitters, dry vermouth, sweet vermouth, vodka, whiskey (rye, bourbon, or blended), gin, tonic water, and fresh lemons.

These drinks are ideas to get the ball rolling. Same as with cooking from recipes, add what you like and ditch what you don't. And let's just cut through all the mixology bullshit—you are most likely drinking to get drunk, and after four drinks it's all gonna taste the same anyway. So if cocktails aren't really your thing, and even if you're post-college and still want to do Jäger shots or drink Alabama Slammers all night, we'll be happy to saddle up to the bar and black out in a super-sloppy way with you.

Same as when **COOKING** from recipes, **ADD** what you like and **DITCH** what **YOU** don't.

We named this drink after one of the greatest movie characters of all time, at least in our house—Max and I quote his famous line to each other all the time. "My name is... (you killed my father, prepare to die)." And well, his name is badass, so why not steal it for a killer cocktail? This drink also utilizes one of the most underrated soda pops in the history of the world. -Eli

Inigo MONTOYA

SERVES 1

ICE CUBES

1½ FL OZ (45 ML) TEQUILA BLANCO

JUICE OF 1 SMALL ORANGE

JUICE OF 1 LIME

SALT

½ CUP (4 FL OZ/125 ML) FRESCA SODA

1. Fill a cocktail shaker and a tall glass with ice. Add the tequila, orange and lime juices, and a pinch of salt to the shaker. Cover and shake. Strain into the glass and top with the Fresca. Give it a stir and serve.

This drink is named for the bartender at my favorite after-work bar, the Narrows, in Bushwick, where Keith makes some of the best drinks in all of Brooklyn. It plays off a classic Manhattan (Eli's favorite drink), replacing the usual bitters with spicy, super-bitter Fernet-Branca, an Italian digestif that the staff of Roberta's might be keeping in business all on their own. -Max

KEITH'S Coc'

SERVES 1

2 FL OZ (60 ML) RYE WHISKEY

1 TBSP SWEET VERMOUTH

5 DASHES FERNET-BRANCA

ICE CUBES

ORANGE TWIST FOR GARNISH

1. Combine the whiskey, vermouth, and Fernet in a cocktail shaker or mixing glass and fill with ice. Cover and shake or use a long-handled bar spoon to mix well. Strain into a cocktail glass or pour into a highball filled with ice. Garnish with the orange twist and serve.

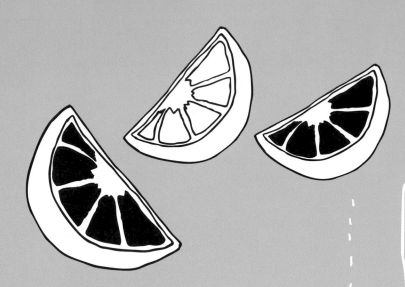

This drink is named after Max, because after working ridiculous hours in the balancing act of managing a kitchen and writing a cookbook, he unwinds with this drink—a spin on the classic Negroni. This version substitutes bourbon for gin and will get you drunk deliciously and efficiently. -Eli

This big drink is a very inexpensive way to get the party going—in other words, a lazy cheapskate's adult punch. Make sure you don't have to work the next day. Around the time this punch is gone, turn to the midnight snacks chapter (page 123) of this book.

Call A CAB

SERVES A CROWD

6 CANS (12 FL OZ/375 ML EACH) LIGHT BEER

2 BOTTLES (20 FL OZ/625 ML EACH) ICED TEA

1 BOTTLE (750 ML) VODKA

1 CONTAINER (12 FL OZ/375 ML) FROZEN LEMONADE CONCENTRATE, THAWED

1 QT (2 LB/1 KG) ICE

1. Mix together all the ingredients in a punch bowl. Serve.

DRUNK to the Max

SERVES 1

ICE CUBES

1½ FL OZ (45 ML) SWEET VERMOUTH

1½ FL OZ (45 ML) CAMPARI

2 FL OZ (60 ML) BOURBON

1 ORANGE SLICE

ORANGE TWIST OR SLICE FOR GARNISH

1. Fill a glass with ice. Pour in the liquors. Squeeze the orange slice into the glass and stir. Garnish with the twist or fresh orange slice and serve.

The Blood TRANSFUSION

SERVES 4-6

1½ CUPS (12 FL OZ/375 ML) VODKA

4 CELERY RIBS, TRIMMED AND CUT IN HALF CROSSWISE, PLUS MORE TRIMMED RIBS FOR GARNISH

12 CHERRY TOMATOES, HALVED, PLUS MORE HALVES FOR GARNISH

10 PEPPERCORNS

1 JALAPEÑO, HALVED AND SEEDED

1 LEMON, HALVED

ICE CUBES

TOMATO JUICE, CHILLED

TABASCO SAUCE

After a night of solid drinking, there are really only two ways to right yourself: get a blood transfusion, or keep on drinking. This Bloody Mary rendition, made with a show-offy infused vodka (steeped in jars packed spectacularly with all the traditional Bloody Mary ingredients), is the perfect drink to serve at a brunch for all your friends. It's like an appetizer for the meal— and since you put in the time (heads up, it needs to sit for at least 5 days), prepare the drinks tableside so you can show how it took so much "hard work" to create.

1. Split the vodka between 2 large Mason jars. Place 2 celery sticks, 6 cherry tomatoes, 5 peppercorns, and a jalapeño half in each jar. Squeeze the juice and flesh of a lemon half into each jar (throw away the peel, that's too bitter). Screw the tops on tightly and put the jars in the back of the refrigerator. Let steep for at least 5 days and up to 2 weeks.

2. To serve, fill 4–6 glasses with ice. Pour about ½ cup (4 fl oz/125 ml) tomato juice into each. Strain 2 or 3 fl oz (60 or 90 ml) of the infused vodka into each glass. Give each glass 2 dashes of Tabasco. Stir with a long-handled bar spoon. Garnish each glass with a few tomato halves and a celery stick, and serve.

DETROIT IS FAMOUS FOR ITS GREEK-AMERICAN DINERS
CALLED CONEY ISLANDS. THESE SPOTS TRANSCEND GEOGRAPHY,
RACE, INCOME, AGE . . . PRACTICALLY EVERYONE WHO LIVES THERE
IS OBSESSED WITH THEM. WHENEVER I TOOK A RED-EYE FROM L.A.,
I ALWAYS DROVE STRAIGHT TO THE CONEY ISLAND NEAR MY PARENTS'
HOUSE TO GET A BOWL OF THIS SATISFYING CHICKEN SOUP WITH
EGG AND LEMON, PLUS A CHICKEN-FINGER PITA TO GO. WHO
CARES THAT IT WAS 7 A.M., I HAD TO GET MY CONEY FIX. –ELI

SERVES 6-8

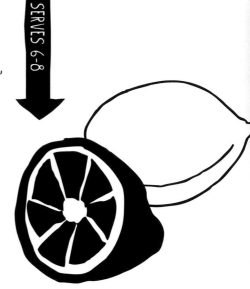

AVGOLEMONO

10 CUPS (80 FL OZ/2.5 L)
GOOD-QUALITY, LOW-
SODIUM CHICKEN BROTH

1 WHOLE CHICKEN,
PREFERABLY ORGANIC,
ABOUT 3 LB (1.5 KG)

1½ CUPS (10½ OZ/330 G)
WHITE RICE

4 LARGE EGG YOLKS

JUICE OF 3 LEMONS

SALT AND FRESHLY
GROUND PEPPER

CHOPPED FRESH FLAT-LEAF
PARSLEY (OPTIONAL)

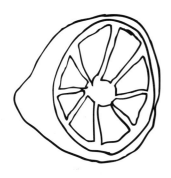

1. Pour the broth into a soup pot. Add the chicken. Cover partially and bring to a boil over high heat. Reduce the heat to low and simmer for 30 minutes. Uncover and use a large spoon to skim off any foam or fat that has risen to the surface. Replace the lid and simmer for 30 minutes longer. Uncover and skim the soup again, then remove from the heat. Using tongs and the large spoon or a large fork, carefully remove the chicken from the broth and place on a platter. Let cool slightly. When cool enough to handle, pull the meat from the bones. Discard the bones and skin and set the meat aside.

2. Meanwhile, add the rice to the soup pot and return to a simmer over low heat. Cook until the rice is tender, about 20 minutes. Return the chicken meat to the soup and remove from the heat. In a heatproof bowl, whisk together the egg yolks until well blended. Using a ladle, scoop some of the soup broth into the bowl of yolks, about ½ cup (4 fl oz/125 ml) at a time, stirring thoroughly after each addition, until you've added about 2 cups (16 fl oz/500 ml) broth total. The egg-broth mixture should be hot to the touch. (Gradually adding the hot broth prevents the eggs from curdling.)

3. Pour the egg-broth mixture back into the pot and stir well. Do not turn on the heat. Stir in the lemon juice. Season with salt and pepper to taste. Ladle the soup into individual bowls, garnish with parsley, if you like, and serve right away.

NOTE If the soup cools and you need to reheat it, be sure you reheat gently over low heat. Don't let the soup come to a boil, or the eggs may curdle.

A LEG OF LAMB, RUBBED WITH HERBS AND SPICES AND ROASTED TO A PERFECT MEDIUM-RARE—SERVED UP WITH CHUNKS OF FRIED EGGPLANT—IS A BEAUTIFUL THING TO BEHOLD. WHEN YOU CUT INTO THE ROAST, YOU REVEAL YOUR SUCCESS AT THE ANCIENT ART OF MEAT COOKERY. IF YOU DO IT RIGHT, ANXIETY DISSOLVES INTO OVERWHELMING PRIDE. NO PRESSURE THOUGH.

roasted leg of LAMB

I BONE-IN LEG OF LAMB, ABOUT 5 LB (2.5 KG)

FOR THE MARINADE

4 LARGE GARLIC CLOVES, CRUSHED BUT LEFT WHOLE

2 TBSP KOSHER SALT

I TBSP GROUND CUMIN

2 TSP GROUND CORIANDER

ZEST OF 2 LEMONS

ZEST OF I ORANGE

2 TSP RED PEPPER FLAKES

¼ CUP (2 FL OZ/60 ML) EXTRA-VIRGIN OLIVE OIL

OLIVE OIL FOR FRYING

2 CUPS (10 OZ/315 G) ALL-PURPOSE FLOUR

2 TBSP ZA'ATAR (PAGE 154)

3 LARGE EGGS

2 CUPS (8 OZ/250 G) PLAIN DRIED BREAD CRUMBS

I LARGE GLOBE EGGPLANT, PEELED AND CUT INTO I-INCH (2.5-CM) CUBES

CHOPPED RED ONION AND FRESH MINT FOR GARNISH

1. Place the lamb in a large roasting pan. Combine all of the marinade ingredients in a bowl and stir to mix well. Rub the marinade evenly all over the lamb. Cover with plastic wrap and let marinate in the refrigerator for at least 1 hour and up to 24 hours.

2. Preheat the oven to 450°F (230°C). Remove the lamb from the fridge and let come to room temperature while the oven is heating; discard the garlic. Roast until the surface of the meat is beginning to caramelize, about 15 minutes. Reduce the oven temperature to 325°F (165°C) and continue roasting until an instant-read thermometer inserted into the thickest part of the lamb, but away from the bone, registers 135°F (57°C) for medium-rare, 30–45 minutes longer. Transfer the lamb to a cutting board, cover with foil, and let rest for 10–15 minutes. Set aside the pan with the drippings.

3. While the lamb is resting, pour olive oil into a large frying pan to a depth of 1 inch (2.5 cm) and heat over medium heat. In a bowl, whisk together the flour and za'atar. Put the eggs in a second bowl and beat until well blended. Put the bread crumbs in a third bowl. Working in batches and using your hands or a slotted spoon, toss the eggplant cubes in the flour, then the eggs, then the bread crumbs until nicely coated on all sides. When the oil is hot, add some of the breaded eggplant cubes, being sure not to crowd the pan. Fry, turning as needed, until uniformly golden brown on all sides, about 20 seconds per side. Transfer to paper towels to drain as they finish. Repeat to cook the remaining eggplant.

4. Carve the lamb, first slicing it from the bone in large pieces, as few as possible. Cut the meat on the diagonal against the grain into slices about ½ inch (12 mm) thick. Place a few slices on each plate, drizzle the pan juices over the top, and arrange the breaded eggplant cubes alongside. Garnish with the red onion and mint. Serve right away.

ORZO
salad

IF YOU ARE IN A BIND TO FIND ORZO, PENNE OR COUSCOUS IS A PERFECTLY ACCEPTABLE SUBSTITUTE. THIS SALAD IS ALSO GOOD SERVED CHILLED—IN FACT, IF YOU LET IT HANG OUT IN THE FRIDGE FOR A BIT, THE FLAVORS WILL HAVE MORE TIME TO MARRY.

SALT AND FRESHLY GROUND PEPPER

1½ CUPS (10½ OZ/330 G) DRIED ORZO

FOR THE VINAIGRETTE

½ CUP (½ OZ/15 G) CHOPPED FRESH FLAT-LEAF PARSLEY

3 TBSP EXTRA-VIRGIN OLIVE OIL

2 TBSP FRESH LEMON JUICE

1 CUP (6 OZ/185 G) CHERRY TOMATOES, HALVED

1 ENGLISH CUCUMBER, DICED

1 RED ONION, DICED

1 CUP (5 OZ/155 G) CRUMBLED FETA CHEESE

½ CUP (2½ OZ/75 G) KALAMATA OLIVES, PITTED

JUICE OF 2 LEMONS

½ CUP (4 FL OZ/125 ML) EXTRA-VIRGIN OLIVE OIL

1. Bring a large pot of generously salted water to a boil over high heat. Add the orzo and cook until al dente, according to package directions. Drain thoroughly and set aside.

2. To make the vinaigrette, put the parsley in a blender. With the machine running, slowly drizzle the 3 Tbsp olive oil through the food tube in a steady stream. Process until all of the oil is added and a smooth purée forms, stopping the machine to scrape down the sides of the jar as needed. Just before mixing with the pasta, add the 2 Tbsp lemon juice and salt and pepper to taste and process until emulsified.

3. Put the orzo in a large serving bowl. Add the vinaigrette and toss until well coated. Add the tomatoes, cucumber, onion, feta, olives, lemon juice, and the ½ cup olive oil and toss gently to mix well. Taste and adjust the seasoning. Serve right away.

FRUIT IS OFTEN MADE TO PLAY THE ROLE OF SIDEKICK TO A LEAD DESSERT LIKE A CAKE. DON'T MARGINALIZE A BEAUTIFUL PIECE OF FRUIT BY PLOPPING IT OVER STORE-BOUGHT ICE CREAM. IF YOU BUY GREAT-QUALITY FIGS AND MAKE THIS RECIPE, YOU CAN ELEVATE THE "PLAIN OLD FRUIT" TO THE FOCAL POINT OF THE PLATE.

grilled figs with burnt HONEY and Pistachio YoGURT

½ CUP (6 OZ/185 G) HONEY

1 TBSP FRESH LEMON JUICE

OLIVE OIL FOR BRUSHING

12 RIPE BLACK MISSION FIGS

¼ CUP (2 OZ/60 G) GREEK YOGURT

½ CUP (2 OZ/60 G) ROASTED PISTACHIOS

1. In a frying pan over medium heat, warm the honey. Cook gently, stirring, until the honey caramelizes and darkens slightly, 5–10 minutes. Remove from the heat, stir in the lemon juice, and set aside.

2. Build a medium-hot fire in a charcoal grill or preheat a gas grill to medium-high. Using a grill brush, scrape the heated grill rack clean. Rub the grill rack with olive oil.

3. Cut the figs in half lengthwise and brush the cut sides with olive oil. Arrange, cut side down, on the grill rack and grill until nicely grill-marked and just tender, 3–5 minutes.

4. To serve, spread the yogurt on a serving plate and tuck the grilled fig halves in it. Drizzle the burnt honey over the top and garnish everything with the roasted pistachios. Serve right away.

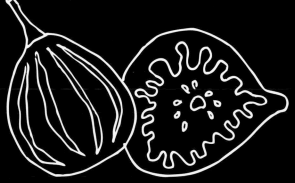

SERVES 4

FISH TACOS with tomatillo salsa

8 CORN TORTILLAS

2 LB (1 KG) FRESH (NOT FROZEN) TILAPIA FILLETS

1 TBSP CHIPOTLE CHILE POWDER

SALT

3 TBSP VEGETABLE OIL

TOMATILLO SALSA (PAGE 19) FOR SERVING

LIME WEDGES FOR SERVING

1. Preheat the oven to 200°F (95°C). Wrap the tortillas in a clean kitchen towel and place in the oven to warm.

2. Sprinkle the fish on both sides with the chile powder and 1 Tbsp salt. In a large frying pan, heat the oil over high heat. When the oil is hot, arrange the fillets in the pan without crowding. Cook, without disturbing, for 2 minutes. Using a wide spatula, flip the fish and cook until opaque throughout, about 2 minutes longer. Flake open one of the fillets in the thickest part with the tip of a sharp knife to check that it's cooked through.

3. Remove the fish from the heat and break it into large chunks. Place 2 warm tortillas on each of 4 plates. Place the fish on top of the tortillas, dividing it evenly. Spoon the salsa over the top and serve right away with lime wedges.

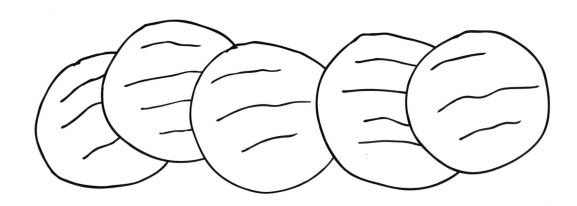

RHETORICAL QUESTION:
WHAT'S BETTER
THAN BEING OUTSIDE
WITH FRIENDS,
EATING TACOS
AND DRINKING BEER?
OBVIOUSLY, NOTHING.

ROASTED corn Soup

WE STARTED TESTING THIS RECIPE EARLY ONE MORNING BUT MAX HAD TO GO INTO WORK BEFORE IT WAS DONE COOKING. HE TEXTED ME A FEW HOURS LATER—"HOW DID THE SOUP TURN OUT?"—AND I TEXTED HIM BACK: "I NOW KNOW WHAT IT FEELS LIKE TO OPEN PRESENTS ON CHRISTMAS MORNING." –ELI

2 RIPE BUT FIRM TOMATOES

KERNELS FROM 6 EARS FRESH CORN (ABOUT 3 CUPS/18 OZ/560 G)

2 RED BELL PEPPERS

1 YELLOW ONION, CHOPPED

1 RED ONION, CHOPPED

3 GARLIC CLOVES, MINCED

ABOUT 2½ CUPS (20 FL OZ/625 ML) GOOD-QUALITY, LOW-SODIUM CHICKEN BROTH, OR MORE AS NEEDED

1 TSP CHIPOTLE CHILE POWDER

SALT

1 CUP (8 FL OZ/250 ML) HEAVY CREAM

SLICED AVOCADO FOR GARNISH

EXTRA-VIRGIN OLIVE OIL FOR DRIZZLING

PAPRIKA FOR GARNISH

1. Preheat the oven to 375°F (190°C). Put the tomatoes in a lightly greased glass baking dish and roast until the skins darken and the tomatoes are caramelized, about 30 minutes. Remove from the oven and let cool. Keep the oven on.

2. Spread the corn in a single layer on a baking sheet and roast until the edges begin to turn golden brown, 10–15 minutes. Meanwhile, when the tomatoes are cool enough to handle, peel off the skins and discard. Set the flesh, with the juices, aside in the baking dish. Remove the corn from the oven and set aside to cool.

3. Place 1 bell pepper on each of 2 gas burners. Turn the burners on high and sear the peppers directly over the flame, using tongs to turn as needed, until the skins are blackened all over, 10–15 minutes total. (Or place under the broiler and broil, turning as needed, until charred and blistered on all sides, about 15 minutes.) Transfer to a brown paper bag and close tightly. Let stand for 15 minutes, then remove the peppers from the bag and remove and discard the skins, core, and seeds.

4. In a soup pot, combine the tomatoes, bell peppers, onions, garlic, and corn, reserving a handful of roasted corn for garnish. Add just enough chicken broth to cover the vegetables and bring to a boil over high heat. Reduce the heat to medium-high and cook until the vegetables are very tender, about 10 minutes. Stir in the chile powder and 2 Tbsp salt. Using an immersion blender, blend the soup until smooth. While blending, slowly drizzle in the cream. Ladle into individual bowls and garnish each portion with a couple of slices of avocado, a few drops of olive oil, a scattering of the reserved roasted corn, and a sprinkle of paprika. Serve hot.

THIS IS ONE OF THOSE RECIPES THAT YOU'LL QUICKLY FIND YOURSELF MAKING ALL THE TIME BECAUSE IT GOES WITH SO MANY MEALS. IT'S SUPER EASY, AND COLESLAW FILLS PLATES AND STOMACHS FOR RIDICULOUSLY LITTLE MONEY. AND IF THERE ARE LEFTOVERS IT'S GREAT ON ANY TYPE OF SANDWICH YOU COULD POSSIBLY IMAGINE. SEE PAGE 134 FOR MORE OF OUR AWESOME SANDWICH IDEAS.

Jalapeño COLESLAW

SERVES 6-8

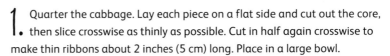

1 HEAD GREEN CABBAGE

1 JALAPEÑO

2 TBSP WHITE VINEGAR

JUICE OF 2 LEMONS

JUICE OF 2 LIMES

SALT AND FRESHLY GROUND PEPPER

AVOCADO CHUNKS FOR GARNISH (OPTIONAL)

1. Quarter the cabbage. Lay each piece on a flat side and cut out the core, then slice crosswise as thinly as possible. Cut in half again crosswise to make thin ribbons about 2 inches (5 cm) long. Place in a large bowl.

2. Using a mandoline or a very sharp knife, slice the jalapeño into paper-thin slices. Add the chile slices and any seeds that escaped to the bowl with the cabbage.

3. Add the vinegar, lemon and lime juices, 1 Tbsp salt, and 1 tsp pepper and toss to mix well. Cover and refrigerate for 1 hour to allow the flavors to marry. Bring to room temperature and taste and adjust the seasonings, then top with avocados, if desired, before serving.

A CHURRO PROVIDES THE SAME SATISFACTION AS A DOUGHNUT, BUT REQUIRES A LOT LESS WORK TO MAKE. USE A PASTRY BAG AND STAR TIP IF YOU WANT THEM TO LOOK AUTHENTIC. BUT SINCE THESE TASTE AMAZING NO MATTER WHAT, YOU CAN ALWAYS FILL A ZIPPERED PLASTIC BAG, CUT OFF THE CORNER, AND PIPE RIGHT INTO THE OIL, OR DROP THEM IN FREE-FORM. —MAX

cinnamon CHURROS

SERVES 4-6 →

½ CUP (4 OZ/125 G) SUGAR, PLUS 1 TBSP

2 TBSP GROUND CINNAMON

VEGETABLE OR CANOLA OIL FOR FRYING

½ CUP (4 OZ/125 G) UNSALTED BUTTER, CUT INTO CUBES

½ TSP SALT

1 CUP (5 OZ/155 G) ALL-PURPOSE FLOUR

4 LARGE EGGS

1. In a bowl, stir together the ½ cup (4 oz/125 g) sugar and the cinnamon. Pour onto a plate and set aside.

2. Pour oil into a large, deep frying pan to a depth of 2 inches (5 cm) and heat until it reaches 350°F (180°C) on a deep-frying thermometer.

3. While the oil is heating, in a saucepan, combine 1 cup (8 fl oz/250 ml) water, the butter, the 1 Tbsp sugar, and the salt and bring to a boil over medium-high heat. When the butter has melted completely, add the flour all at once. Using a wooden spoon, beat vigorously until all of the flour is incorporated and the dough forms a ball that sticks to itself. Immediately remove from the heat and let cool for about 2 minutes.

4. When the flour mixture has cooled slightly, beat in the eggs, 1 at a time, mixing well to incorporate each egg before adding the next. When the last egg is fully incorporated, scrape the dough into a large pastry bag fitted with a large star tip. Carefully squeeze the dough directly into the hot oil, making strips about 4 inches (10 cm) long. Working in batches if necessary, fry, turning every few minutes with tongs, until deep golden brown on all sides and cooked through, 5–7 minutes total. Transfer to paper towels to drain briefly, then immediately toss in the cinnamon sugar. Serve right away.

WE BOTH LOVE OYSTERS. AND EVERYTHING IS BETTER FRIED.
THIS IS A GREAT DISH THAT SEEMS MORE COMPLICATED THAN IT IS.
SURPRISINGLY, THE FRIED FLAVOR AND THE AIOLI DON'T OVERSHADOW THE
OYSTERS. EVERYTHING STANDS UP WELL ON ITS OWN. WE SERVE THESE AS
A PLATED APPETIZER AT PARTIES, BUT YOU CAN EASILY TURN THEM INTO
A SANDWICH BY CUTTING THE BRIOCHE INTO BIGGER SLICES.

SERVES 4

fried OYSTER bites

2 CUPS (16 FL OZ/500 ML)
BUTTERMILK

8 FRESH MEDIUM OYSTERS,
SHUCKED

2 TBSP UNSALTED BUTTER

2 SLICES BRIOCHE,
QUARTERED

VEGETABLE OIL FOR FRYING

1 CUP (5 OZ/155 G)
ALL-PURPOSE FLOUR

SEA SALT

SPICY AIOLI (PAGE 154)

2 GREEN ONIONS,
WHITE AND TENDER GREEN
PARTS ONLY, THINLY SLICED
ON THE DIAGONAL

1. Pour the buttermilk into a bowl. Add the oysters and push to submerge in the milk. Cover and refrigerate until ready to use.

2. In a frying pan over medium heat, melt 1 Tbsp of the butter and use a spatula to spread it evenly around the pan bottom. Place the brioche pieces in the hot butter and cook until golden brown on the bottom, about 2 minutes. Using tongs, flip each piece over. Add the remaining 1 Tbsp butter and cook the bread until golden brown on the second side, about 2 minutes longer. Transfer to a plate and set aside.

3. Pour oil into a saucepan to a depth of 3 inches (7.5 cm) and heat over medium-high heat until it reaches 350°F (180°C) on a deep-frying thermometer. Reduce the heat as needed to maintain the temperature. Meanwhile, put the flour in a bowl. Using a slotted spoon, remove the oysters from the buttermilk, letting some of the milk drip off, and transfer to the flour. Toss to coat completely. Lift the oysters from the flour with tongs, shake off the excess, and place carefully in the hot oil. Fry until golden brown, stirring occasionally, 2–4 minutes. Using the slotted spoon, transfer to paper towels to drain. Sprinkle with salt while still warm. To assemble, spread a teaspoon or so of the aioli on each piece of brioche. Sprinkle each with green onions, then place an oyster on top. Serve right away.

THIS RECIPE COMPLETELY BLOWS UP ANY LINGERING IDEA OF A PORK CHOP AS A FLAVORLESS HUNK OF CHEWY MEAT. THE BRINE IS ESSENTIAL TO DEVELOP THE FLAVOR. THE THICKNESS OF THE CHOP ALLOWS YOU TO COOK IT SO THAT WHEN SLICED IT'S A PERFECT JUICY PINK ON THE INSIDE.

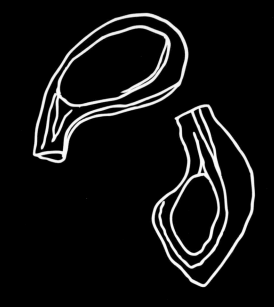

PORK CHOPS

SERVES 6-8 ➡ ## With apple chutney

FOR THE BRINE

⅔ CUP (5 OZ/155 G) SUGAR

⅔ CUP (5 OZ/155 G) SALT

1 FRESH THYME SPRIG

1 FRESH ROSEMARY SPRIG

1 TSP WHOLE BLACK PEPPERCORNS

1 TSP CORIANDER SEEDS

ICE CUBES

3 BONE-IN, DOUBLE-CUT PORK CHOPS, ABOUT 4 LB (1.8 KG) TOTAL WEIGHT

1 TBSP CANOLA OIL

2 TBSP UNSALTED BUTTER

1 FRESH ROSEMARY SPRIG

1 FRESH THYME SPRIG

1 GARLIC CLOVE, CRUSHED

APPLE CHUTNEY (PAGE 153) FOR SERVING

1. To make the brine, in a large saucepan, bring 2 qt (2 l) water to a boil over high heat. Add the sugar and salt and stir until dissolved. Stir in the herb sprigs, peppercorns, and coriander seeds and remove from the heat. Add about 2 qt (4 lb/2 kg) ice and stir to melt. Refrigerate until completely cooled, about 2 hours.

2. Add the pork chops to the brine and weight down with plates or heavy canned goods. Let brine in the fridge for 24 hours. Remove the chops and pat dry with paper towels. Let come to room temperature for at least 1 hour before cooking (this will help the chops cook evenly throughout).

3. In a large frying pan, heat the oil over medium heat. When the oil is hot, sear the chops until they are nicely browned on both sides, about 4 minutes per side. Add the butter to the pan, reduce the heat to medium-low, and let the butter melt. Using a large spoon, baste the chops with butter constantly for about 5 minutes, tilting the pan as needed, and using tongs to flip the chops about every 2 minutes. Add the herb sprigs and garlic clove during the last 2 or 3 minutes of cooking to infuse the pan juices with their flavors. Cook until an instant-read thermometer inserted into the thickest part of each chop away from bone registers 125°F (52°C). Transfer the chops to a platter, cover loosely with foil, and let rest for 10 minutes.

4. To serve, carve the meat off the bone into thick slices. Arrange the slices on dinner plates. Stir any juices left on the platter into the pan sauce and drizzle over the top. Spoon some chutney on top or alongside and serve right away.

ELI'S TIP: COME PREPARED TO DINNER PARTIES WITH A LOT OF MADE UP STORIES.

SERVES 4 ➤

CURLY ENDIVE
with warm anchovy
vinaigrette

THIS IS OUR VARIATION ON THE CLASSIC ITALIAN DISH BAGNA CAUDA, WHICH IS A WARM DIP THAT YOU DUNK VEGETABLES INTO, SIMILAR TO A FONDUE. BUT HERE, INSTEAD OF DIPPING VEGETABLES INTO THE SAUCE, WE'VE DONE IT AS A COMPOSED SALAD DRESSED WITH THE SAUCE AS A VINAIGRETTE.

1 LARGE HEAD CURLY ENDIVE OR ESCAROLE, CORED AND SEPARATED INTO LEAVES

4 FRENCH BREAKFAST RADISHES, TRIMMED AND THINLY SLICED

6 TBSP (3 FL OZ/90 ML) EXTRA-VIRGIN OLIVE OIL

2-OZ (60-G) TIN ANCHOVY FILLETS

1 GARLIC CLOVE, MINCED

½ TSP RED PEPPER FLAKES

3 TBSP FRESH LEMON JUICE

PARMESAN CHEESE SHAVINGS FOR GARNISH

1. Arrange the endive leaves on a platter and scatter the radishes over them.

2. In a frying pan over medium heat, warm 3 Tbsp of the olive oil. Add the anchovies and sauté until they soften and break down, 3–5 minutes. Add the garlic and sauté until lightly golden, about 1 minute longer. Stir in the red pepper flakes and lemon juice and remove from the heat.

3. Immediately scrape the contents of the frying pan into a blender, add the remaining 3 Tbsp olive oil, and process to a smooth purée. Drizzle the warm anchovy vinaigrette over the endive and radishes and scatter the Parmesan shavings over the top. Serve right away.

AFTER WE MAKE A BATCH OF THIS ROMESCO SAUCE,
WE PUT IT ON THINGS LIKE EGGS, GRILLED CHEESE,
AND TURKEY SANDWICHES. WE FIND ANY EXCUSE
WE CAN THINK OF TO DUNK AND COVER STUFF IN THE
INCREDIBLY VERSATILE AND TASTY ROMESCO. —MAX

 SERVES 4

ROASTED ROOT VEGETABLES
With romesco sauce

FOR THE ROMESCO SAUCE

¾ CUP (3 OZ/90 G) RAW ALMONDS

6 PLUM TOMATOES

2 RED BELL PEPPERS

1 YELLOW ONION, CUT INTO SLICES ABOUT ½ INCH (12 MM) THICK

3 GARLIC CLOVES

2 TBSP OLIVE OIL

KOSHER SALT

2 TBSP SHERRY VINEGAR

2 TSP SMOKED PAPRIKA

¼ TSP CAYENNE PEPPER

4 LB (2 KG) MIXED ROOT VEGETABLES SUCH AS CARROTS, PARSNIPS, BEETS, CELERY ROOT, AND SWEET POTATOES, PEELED AND CUT INTO 1½-INCH (4-CM) PIECES

2 TBSP OLIVE OIL

1. To make the romesco, preheat the oven to 375°F (190°C). Spread the almonds on a large, heavy-duty baking sheet and toast in the oven, stirring once or twice, until fragrant and slightly darkened, about 10 minutes. Remove from the oven and immediately pour onto a plate to cool; the nuts can burn easily. Leave the oven on.

2. On the baking sheet, toss the tomatoes, bell peppers, onion slices, and garlic cloves with the 2 Tbsp olive oil and 1 tsp salt. Roast until all the vegetables are tender and slightly charred, 15–30 minutes. As each vegetable is done, transfer it to a bowl. The onions and garlic will cook first, followed by the peppers and then the tomatoes.

3. When all the romesco vegetables are done, transfer them to a blender or food processor. Add the vinegar, paprika, and cayenne and process to a smooth purée. Taste and adjust the seasoning. Set the romesco aside.

4. Clean off the baking sheet, then add the root vegetables and toss with the 2 Tbsp olive oil and 1 tsp salt. Spread the vegetables in a single layer and roast until tender and nicely caramelized, about 40 minutes. Arrange the roasted root vegetables on a platter and pour the romesco sauce over them. Serve right away.

GOING FREE-FORM IS GOOD AND HERE'S WHY:
YOU DON'T HAVE TO PUT IT IN A BAKING DISH AND IT DOESN'T
NEED TO BE PERFECT. WE'RE OVER PERFECT. WHO CARES?
THIS LOOK IS MUCH MORE INTERESTING AND NATURAL AND
SUPER EASY TO MAKE. PEAR AND GINGER IS A GREAT-TASTING
MATCH. WE THREW IN SOME CHEWY CANDIED GINGER,
FOR ANOTHER FLAVOR COMPONENT.

SERVES 4-6 ➡

PEAR Tart

FOR THE DOUGH

2½ CUPS (12½ OZ/390 G)
ALL-PURPOSE FLOUR

¼ CUP (2 OZ/60 G)
GRANULATED SUGAR

PINCH OF SALT

1 CUP (8 OZ/250 G) COLD
UNSALTED BUTTER,
CUT INTO SMALL CUBES

2 LARGE EGG YOLKS

¼ CUP (2 FL OZ/60 ML)
ICE WATER, PLUS MORE
IF NEEDED

FOR THE FILLING

2 PEARS, PEELED, CORED,
AND SLICED

¼ CUP (2 OZ/60 G)
GRANULATED SUGAR

5 LARGE PIECES CANDIED
GINGER, DICED

2 TBSP LIGHT BROWN
SUGAR

1 TBSP GROUND CINNAMON

¼ TSP SALT

1. To make the dough, in a food processor, combine the flour, granulated sugar, and salt. Add the butter pieces and pulse until the mixture looks like a coarse meal, about 20 seconds. In a separate bowl, lightly beat the egg yolks, then beat in the ice water. Turn the food processor on and pour in the egg mixture slowly through the food tube, letting the machine run just until combined. Do not exceed 30 seconds. If the dough is still crumbly, add another tablespoon or so of ice water. Remove the dough from the food processor and wrap in plastic wrap. Refrigerate until well chilled, at least 2 hours or up to 24 hours.

2. When you are ready to assemble the tart, preheat the oven to 375°F (190°C). To make the filling, in a bowl, combine the pears, granulated sugar, candied ginger, brown sugar, cinnamon, and salt and stir to mix well.

3. Unwrap the dough and place on a lightly floured work surface. Roll out the dough to a thickness of about ¼ inch (6 mm). Using a pie or cake pan as a guide, cut out a circle about 10 inches (25 cm) in diameter. Transfer to a greased or parchment-lined baking sheet. Scoop the filling into the middle and spread evenly toward the edges, leaving a 3-inch (7.5-cm) border uncovered. Starting at the bottom edge of the circle nearest you, fold in a pleat of dough about 2 inches (5 cm) wide toward the center and only partly covering the filling. Continue to fold over pleats of dough, moving clockwise, until all of the edges of the dough are folded in. There should be an opening in the center of about 5 inches (13 cm) to show off the filling.

4. Bake the tart until golden brown, about 20 minutes. Let cool for 10 minutes, then cut into wedges and serve.

WHO DOESN'T LOVE CHICKEN SCHNITZEL? MAYBE PEOPLE WHO DON'T LIKE PUPPIES OR RAINBOWS. I DON'T KNOW ANY OF THEM AND I DON'T EVER WANT TO. WE USE SALT-AND-VINEGAR POTATO CHIPS TO ADD A NICE TANGY ELEMENT. —MAX

SERVES 4

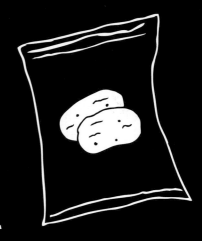

Chicken SCHNITZEL

4 BONELESS, SKINLESS CHICKEN BREAST HALVES (ABOUT 6 OZ/185 G EACH)

3 CUPS (4½ OZ/140 G) PACKED SALT-AND-VINEGAR POTATO CHIPS

2 CUPS (8 OZ/250 G) UNSEASONED DRIED BREAD CRUMBS

2 CUPS (10 OZ/315 G) ALL-PURPOSE FLOUR

4 LARGE EGGS

SALT

CANOLA OR GRAPESEED OIL FOR FRYING

1 TBSP UNSALTED BUTTER

THYME SPAETZLE (PAGE 153) FOR SERVING

1. Wrap a chicken breast half in plastic wrap and place it on a work surface. Using a rolling pin or a small, heavy frying pan, pound the chicken breast to an even thickness of about ¼ inch (6 mm). Repeat to pound the remaining breast halves.

2. Put the potato chips and bread crumbs in a food processor and pulse until finely ground and well mixed. Spread the crumb mixture on a large plate. Spread the flour on another large plate. In a wide, shallow bowl, beat the eggs with a pinch of salt.

3. Dredge a piece of chicken in the flour, then dip into the eggs, turning to coat, and then press each side in the crumb mixture to cover completely. Place on a baking sheet. Repeat to coat the remaining chicken pieces.

4. Set up 2 large frying pans and pour oil into each to a depth of ¼ inch (6 mm). Warm the oil over medium heat, and then place 2 breaded chicken breasts in each pan and cook until golden on the first side, about 4 minutes. Add ½ Tbsp butter to each pan, let melt, and tilt the pan to distribute it evenly. Turn the chicken breasts and add more oil if the pan seems dry. Cook until golden brown on the second side and opaque throughout, about 4 minutes longer. Serve right away with the spaetzle.

braised cabbage with CARROTS and BACON

SERVES 4-6 ↓

WE TOOK A CUE FROM THE MOM MOVE "I'LL TRY ANYTHING TO GET MY KIDS TO EAT VEGETABLES." BACON MAKES EVEN THE MOST INSUFFERABLY VEGGIE-PHOBIC PEOPLE CONSIDER TAKING A BITE. AND THAT ONE BITE IS ALL YOU'LL NEED TO CONVINCE THEM.

8 OZ (250 G) SLICED BACON

1 YELLOW ONION, HALVED AND THINLY SLICED LENGTHWISE

½ HEAD RED CABBAGE, QUARTERED, CORED, AND THINLY SLICED LENGTHWISE

3 CARROTS, PEELED AND GRATED

2 CUPS (16 FL OZ/500 ML) DRY WHITE WINE

3 TBSP WHITE WINE VINEGAR

3 JUNIPER BERRIES, CRUSHED

1 BAY LEAF

SALT

1 TBSP BROWN SUGAR

2 TBSP UNSALTED BUTTER

1. In a large frying pan over medium-low heat, cook the bacon until crisp, turning the strips often so they cook evenly and to render the most fat, 10–15 minutes. Using tongs, transfer to paper towels to drain. Crumble the bacon and set aside.

2. Pour off all but about 2 Tbsp of the fat in the pan and place over medium heat. Add the onion and sauté until tender and lightly golden, about 10 minutes. Add the cabbage, carrots, wine, vinegar, juniper berries, bay leaf, and salt to taste, and stir. Your pan might be quite full, but don't worry, the cabbage will shrink a lot as it cooks and you'll have more room to mix well. Raise the heat to high and bring to a boil, then reduce the heat to low and maintain a gentle simmer. Stir in the brown sugar.

3. Cover the pan and simmer until most of the liquid has evaporated and the vegetables are tender, about 45 minutes. Discard the bay leaf. Taste and adjust the seasoning with salt, if needed. Add the butter and stir to melt. (This "finishes" the dish by uniting the flavors and adding a nice little gloss to the sauce.) Transfer to a serving bowl or individual plates, garnish with the crispy bacon bits, and serve right way.

THIS COOL REFRESHING SALAD GOES PERFECTLY WITH THE HOT, CRUNCHY, CRUSTED SCHNITZEL. IF YOU HAVE ANY LEFTOVERS, ADD IN CHOPPED TOMATOES AND FETA CHEESE FOR A GREAT BREAKFAST SALAD THE NEXT MORNING.

CUCUMBER SALAD

SERVES 4 →

2 LARGE ENGLISH CUCUMBERS, PEELED

1 LARGE RED ONION, PEELED AND TRIMMED

¼ CUP (¼ OZ/7 G) MINCED FRESH DILL

¼ CUP (2 FL OZ/60 ML) FRESH LEMON JUICE, PLUS MORE IF NEEDED

¼ CUP (2 FL OZ/60 ML) EXTRA-VIRGIN OLIVE OIL

SALT AND FRESHLY GROUND PEPPER

1. Using a mandoline or a very sharp chef's knife, cut the cucumbers crosswise into very thin slices. You want the slices to be about the thinness of a credit card, but not translucent. Place the cucumbers in a large bowl.

2. Cut the onion in half through the root end. Place, cut side down, on the mandoline and cut into paper-thin slices, or slice very thinly with the chef's knife. You want the onions to be so thin they are translucent. Add to the bowl with the cucumbers, add the dill, and stir to mix well.

3. In a small bowl or a glass measuring jar, whisk together the lemon juice, olive oil, and salt and pepper. Taste; the strongest flavor should be the lemon juice. If the oil is overpowering, add another tablespoon or two of lemon juice and taste again.

4. Pour the dressing over the cucumber mixture and toss to coat thoroughly. Refrigerate until well chilled, at least 30 minutes and up to 2 hours. Just before serving, taste and adjust the seasoning. Serve with a slotted spoon, letting the salad drain briefly before plating.

IT SEEMED LIKE WE HAD ENOUGH ALMONDS AT OUR APARTMENT TO LAST A YEAR. NEITHER MAX NOR I REMEMBERED EVEN BUYING THEM. (SOMETIMES WE BLACK OUT AT THE GROCERY STORE.) A FEW DAYS LATER WE NEEDED TO WRITE A DESSERT RECIPE. "OH NICE DUDE—LET'S USE ALL THOSE ALMONDS." SO WE MADE SOME ALMOND COOKIES. AND THEN WE ATE THE ENTIRE BATCH BEFORE THEY EVEN HIT THE COOLING RACK. NAH, WE WEREN'T DRUNK. JUST FAT. —ELI

MAKES 20 COOKIES

ALMOND cookies

1½ CUPS (6 OZ/185 G) WHOLE ALMONDS, PLUS SLICED ALMONDS FOR GARNISH

1 CUP (8 OZ/250 G) SUGAR

½ CUP (4 OZ/125 G) UNSALTED BUTTER, MELTED

1 LARGE EGG

1 CUP (4 OZ/125 G) ALL-PURPOSE FLOUR

1 TSP PURE VANILLA EXTRACT

1. Preheat the oven to 375°F (190°C). Put the almonds in a food processor and process until coarsely ground, 15–20 seconds. Stop the machine and pulse carefully until the nuts are finely and uniformly ground, stirring in between pulses as needed. Work carefully, as you don't want the nuts to turn to paste. Set aside.

2. In a large bowl, combine the sugar and melted butter and stir to mix well. Beat in the egg, then add the flour and the ground almonds and mix well. Stir in the vanilla extract.

3. Scoop out 1 Tbsp of dough, roll it into a ball between your palms, and then flatten into a round cookie. Place on a greased baking sheet. Repeat with the remaining dough, spacing the cookies about 2 inches (5 cm) apart on the pan. You may need 2 baking sheets.

4. Arrange 3 almond slices in the center of each cookie, tucking them in at a slight angle. Bake until lightly golden brown, 9–10 minutes. Remove from the oven and allow to cool on a baking rack.

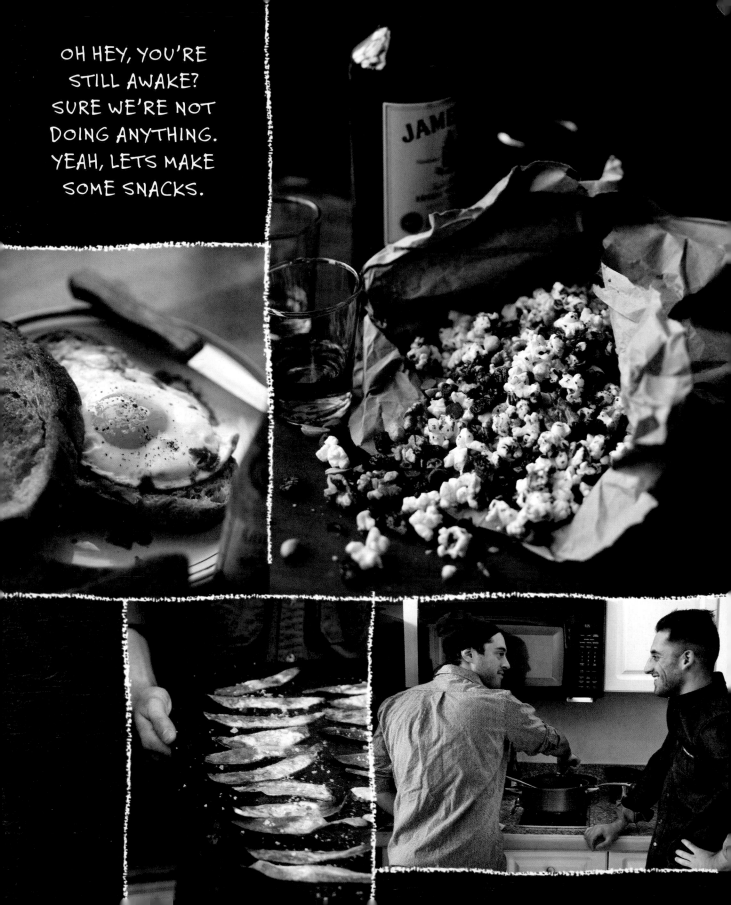

OH HEY, YOU'RE STILL AWAKE? SURE WE'RE NOT DOING ANYTHING. YEAH, LETS MAKE SOME SNACKS.

Midnight Snacks

I LOVE TO COME HOME, BLAST SOME MUSIC, POUR MYSELF A BEVERAGE, AND MAKE A MEATLOAF SANDWICH ON A BAGUETTE WITH A PILE OF THESE FRIES. SINCE THEY AREN'T FRIED, IT'S NOT A SUPER GROSS LATE-NIGHT SNACK. THE THINNESS MAKES THEM CRISPY, SO IT'S REALLY LIKE HALF POTATO CHIP, HALF FRY. AS MY BEST FRIEND SAYS, IT'S ALL ABOUT THE DIPPING SAUCES: BBQ, KETCHUP, HONEY MUSTARD, RANCH, AND SRIRACHA MAYO. —ELI

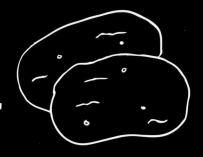

SERVES 1 →

thin-cut fries
FOR ONE

1 POTATO, PREFERABLY RUSSET

OLIVE OIL FOR GREASING

COARSE SALT AND FRESHLY GROUND PEPPER

CHILI POWDER (OPTIONAL)

BBQ SAUCE, KETCHUP, HONEY MUSTARD, RANCH DRESSING, AND/OR SRIRACHA MAYO (MIX SRIRACHA SAUCE AND MAYO TOGETHER) FOR SERVING

1. Preheat the broiler.

2. Quarter the potato lengthwise and turn each piece on the cutting board so the largest flat side is down. Using a very sharp chef's knife, cut the potato lengthwise into very thin slices. You want the slices to be about the thinness of a credit card, but not translucent.

3. Using a paper towel, coat a baking sheet lightly with olive oil. Arrange the potato slices on the pan in a single layer. Do not overlap. Sprinkle with salt and pepper. For spicy fries, sprinkle with chili powder.

4. Place under the broiler. After 7–10 minutes, the fries should be beginning to brown. This is a good thing. After 10 minutes, remove the fries from the oven. Using metal tongs (you need thin edges), gently grasp the end of each fry and flip over. You may rip a few and lose a couple to sticking. Don't worry; this is just what happens. When all the fries are flipped, return to the broiler. Broil the second side just until browned, 1–2 minutes longer, watching carefully so you do not let them burn. Remove from the oven immediately. Sprinkle with a little more salt and eat warm, with the dipping sauces.

ASIAN FOOD IS GOD'S GIFT TO LATE-NIGHT SNACKING. IT'S SALTY AND SWEET AND FILLING. AS THE ETERNAL DEBATE RAGES ON ABOUT WHETHER "SOAKING UP BOOZE" CAN HELP AVOID A HANGOVER, EVERYONE CAN AGREE THAT RICE WITH EGGS AND VEGGIES IS DELICIOUS. A QUICK STIR-FRY IS IN A LOT OF PEOPLE'S WHEELHOUSE. THIS FRIED RICE IS JUST AS EASY BUT TASTES WAY BETTER.

fried RICE

3 LARGE EGGS

5 TBSP (3 FL OZ/80 ML) VEGETABLE OIL

1 CARROT, PEELED AND DICED

1 CUP (5 OZ/155 G) FROZEN PEAS, THAWED

2 CUPS (10 OZ/315 G) STEAMED RICE (COOKED ACCORDING TO PACKAGE DIRECTIONS AND COOLED)

2 TBSP SOY SAUCE, PLUS MORE IF NEEDED

THINLY SLICED GREEN ONIONS FOR GARNISH

1. In a small bowl, beat the eggs. In a medium frying pan, heat 1 Tbsp of the oil over medium heat. Add the eggs and stir until cooked but still moist, scraping the bottom and tilting the pan as you work to cook them evenly. Scrape into a bowl and set aside.

2. In a large frying pan or wok, heat 2 Tbsp of the oil over medium-high heat. Add the carrot and peas and sauté until softened and all the vegetables are nicely browned here and there, about 3 minutes. Scrape into a bowl and set aside.

3. Using the same pan you cooked the vegetables in, heat the remaining 2 Tbsp oil over high heat. Add the rice, spread it evenly in the pan, and do not touch it for 2 minutes. Using a wide spatula or 2 spatulas, flip the rice as best you can and fry the other side for 2 minutes longer. Switch to a wooden spoon, and toss and stir the rice for another 2 minutes. It will be slightly crispy to the touch.

4. Add the egg and vegetables to the rice and mix well. Cook to warm through, about 30 seconds. Add the 2 Tbsp soy sauce. Taste. If it is not sufficiently delicious, add additional soy sauce, 1 Tbsp at a time. Spoon onto plates or into bowls and garnish with the green onions. Serve right away.

BET YOU'VE SEEN THE COMMERCIALS FOR ALL THOSE GROSS MICROWAVABLE PASTA-IN-POUCHES. YOU KNOW WHAT THOSE TASTE LIKE? LAZINESS AND SHAME. WE HOPE YOU RESPECT YOURSELF MORE THAN PUTTING THAT STUFF IN YOUR BODY, EVEN LATE AT NIGHT. MAKE THIS DISH INSTEAD. MAKE EXTRA, REHEAT IT AT WORK THE NEXT DAY, AND SPRINKLE SOME FRESH PARM OVER THE TOP. COWORKER JEALOUSY COMMENCE. (TIP—IF YOU HAVE LEFTOVER MEATBALLS, PAGE 43, USE THEM HERE.)

kitchen sink PASTA

SERVES 2

SALT AND FRESHLY GROUND PEPPER

3 TBSP OLIVE OIL

1 GARLIC CLOVE, MINCED

2 CUPS (12 OZ/375 G) DICED VEGETABLES SUCH AS ZUCCHINI, MUSHROOMS, TOMATOES, ONIONS, BELL PEPPERS, BROCCOLI, AND/OR SNAP PEAS

1 TBSP UNSALTED BUTTER

PINCH OF DRIED OREGANO OR THYME (OPTIONAL)

1 CUP (4-7 OZ/125-220 G) DRIED PASTA, ANY NOODLE OR SHAPE YOU LIKE

FRESHLY GRATED PARMESAN CHEESE FOR SERVING

1. Bring a large pot of generously salted water to a boil over high heat.

2. In a frying pan, heat the olive oil over medium heat. Add the garlic and sauté for 1 minute. Add the vegetables and sauté until they are tender and beginning to brown, about 5 minutes.

3. Add the butter and let melt, then stir to mix well. Season with salt and pepper to taste. Add a pinch of oregano, if you like.

4. Cook the pasta until al dente, according to package directions. Drain well. Return the pasta to the warm pot and add the vegetables. Stir gently to mix well.

5. Divide the pasta and vegetables among plates and serve right away with plenty of Parmesan.

pop pppop pop. pop!

In L.A. I had a roommate who was addicted to popcorn legit. For more than a year, I never saw her go a day without eating it. And who can blame her? As we'll show you, popcorn is the perfect canvas for any ingredient. She was a master of making popcorn fit into any part of her day because for her, popcorn was the ideal side dish, snack, or dessert. As a true comfort food, popcorn gave her a shoulder to cry on after a hard day. Popcorn was always there for her and, unlike her roommate, popcorn never rolled its eyes and told her she'd never get married. With these different flavor variations, you too should be able to make popcorn your new best friend.

Popcorn is really cheap, incredibly fast, and can take on any flavor—sweet, salty, savory, sour. If you're looking for a snack or side dish to feed 1 or 20, there's nothing better than making some popcorn and pouring whatever you can find in the fridge or cupboard on top. Everybody knows you can't go wrong with butter and salt but here are some other tasty options. –Eli

tip For those of you poor college (or poor post-college) students out there looking for a personal homemade gift for a birthday or the holidays, go to a Salvation Army and find a nice wooden or tin box. Clean it really well, line it with parchment paper, and fill it with homemade popcorn. It's personal, edible, and looks like you actually put some time into it. And no one will know it cost you less than a movie ticket.

basic popcorn

SERVES 1-2

1 TBSP CANOLA OIL

½ CUP (3 OZ/90 G) POPCORN KERNELS

1. Pour the oil into a saucepan with a tight-fitting lid and pop the popcorn per the package directions, or pop in a microwave if using microwave popcorn. Place the popped corn in a large bowl.

HIPPIE Popcorn

2 TBSP BUTTER, MELTED

1 BOWL BASIC POPCORN (PAGE 128)

¼ CUP (¾ OZ/20 G) NUTRITIONAL YEAST

2-3 TBSP SOY SAUCE

1 TBSP GRANULATED GARLIC

1. Drizzle 1 Tbsp of the butter over the popcorn and toss to mix. Add the remaining 1 Tbsp butter and toss again to mix well. Sprinkle with the nutritional yeast, 2 Tbsp of the soy sauce, and the granulated garlic and toss until evenly distributed. Taste and add more soy sauce, if desired. Eat right away.

SPICY Chili-Citrus Popcorn

JUICE OF 1 LEMON AND 1 LIME

1 BOWL BASIC POPCORN (PAGE 128)

¼ TSP CHILI POWDER

1 TBSP GRANULATED GARLIC

1. In a small bowl, stir together the lemon and lime juices. Drizzle over the popcorn and toss to mix well.

2. Sprinkle the chili powder and granulated garlic over the popcorn and toss until evenly distributed. Eat right away.

APPLE-CINNAMON popcorn

1 APPLE, FINELY DICED

1 TBSP BUTTER, MELTED

1 BOWL BASIC POPCORN (PAGE 128)

2 TBSP GROUND CINNAMON

1 TBSP SUGAR

1. Add the apple and melted butter to the popcorn and toss to mix well. Sprinkle the cinnamon and sugar over the popcorn and toss until evenly distributed. Eat right away.

TRAIL Mix Popcorn

2 TBSP BUTTER, MELTED

1 BOWL BASIC POPCORN (PAGE 128)

½ CUP (2 OZ/60 G) DRIED CRANBERRIES

½ CUP (2½ OZ/75 G) SALTED PEANUTS

¼ CUP (1½ OZ/45 G) CHOCOLATE CHIPS

2 TBSP PURE MAPLE SYRUP

1. Drizzle the melted butter over the popcorn and toss to mix. Add the cranberries, nuts, and chocolate chips and toss until evenly distributed.

2. Drizzle the maple syrup over and toss to mix well. Eat right away.

I AM COMPLETELY AND HIGHLY ILLOGICALLY WEIRDED OUT BY BREAKFAST AT NIGHT. YOU COULD WAKE ME UP AT ANY HOUR OF THE DAY AND I'LL GLADLY CONSUME A TURKEY SANDWICH BUT I CAN'T WRAP MY HEAD AROUND PANCAKES FOR DINNER. REGARDLESS OF MY PERSONAL CONVICTIONS, I'VE HEARD FROM MULTIPLE REPUTABLE SOURCES THAT LATE-NIGHT BREAKFAST IS WHAT'S HOT ON THE STREETS. SO IN THE SPIRIT OF GIVING THE PEOPLE WHAT THEY WANT, I PRESENT TO YOU A MIDNIGHT FRITTATA. —ELI

SERVES 4-6 →

farmers' market Frittata

4 LARGE EGGS

¼ CUP (2 FL OZ/60 ML) WHOLE MILK

SALT AND FRESHLY GROUND PEPPER

2 TBSP OLIVE OIL

1 CUP (4 OZ/125 G) CHOPPED FRESH SEASONAL VEGETABLES SUCH AS TOMATOES, BELL PEPPERS, ASPARAGUS, ONIONS, EGGPLANT IN ANY COMBINATION

4 STRIPS BACON OR 3 OZ (90 G) HAM OR PANCETTA, CHOPPED (ABOUT ½ CUP)

½ CUP (2 OZ/60 G) FRESHLY GRATED PARMESAN CHEESE

1 TBSP MINCED FRESH FLAT-LEAF PARSLEY (OPTIONAL)

1. Preheat the broiler.

2. In a bowl, beat together the eggs, milk, 1 tsp salt, and ½ tsp pepper. In an ovenproof frying pan over medium heat, warm the olive oil. When the oil is hot, add the vegetables and sauté until tender and beginning to brown, about 3 minutes. Scrape the vegetables onto a plate and set aside.

3. Using the same pan over medium heat, cook the chopped bacon until crisp, about 5 minutes for bacon or 2 minutes for precooked ham. Return the vegetables to the pan and spread in an even layer. Pour in the egg mixture evenly around the pan and cook without disturbing until the egg mixture sets, about 5 minutes.

4. Transfer the pan to the oven and broil until golden brown, about 3 minutes. Remove from the oven and sprinkle the Parmesan over the top, then return to the oven and broil for 1 minute longer to melt the cheese. Sprinkle with the parsley, if using. Cut into wedges or scoop from the pan and serve right away.

WHAT'S MORE PERFECT THAN THE SIMPLICITY OF THIS
SANDWICH? IT'S COMFORTING, NOT TOO DIFFICULT TO MAKE,
AND YOU NEED ONLY A FEW KEY INGREDIENTS. THESE ARE
THE ESSENTIALS TO PREPARING THE KIND OF MIDNIGHT FOOD
WE LOVE. THE KIND OF FOOD THAT WILL MAKE YOU CLOSE
YOUR EYES AND EXHALE A HOT CHEESY JUMBLE THAT SOUNDS
SOMETHING LIKE "OH MY GAH SO FREAKIN' GOOD."

FRIED EGG ← SERVES 1
sandwich

8 THIN SLICES
CHEDDAR CHEESE

2 THICK SLICES
SOURDOUGH BREAD

1 TBSP OLIVE OIL

1 LARGE EGG

SALT AND FRESHLY
GROUND PEPPER

HOT SAUCE FOR SERVING

1. Preheat the broiler.

2. Put 4 of the cheese slices on each piece of bread and put them
on a baking sheet, cheese side up. Slide the pan under the broiler.
Let the cheese melt while you cook the egg, but keep an eye on
the broiler, because the cheese can burn fast.

3. While the cheese is melting, heat the olive oil in a frying pan over
medium high heat. After about 20 seconds, crack the egg into the
pan. Reduce the heat to medium and let the egg sit until the white sets
completely. Sprinkle with salt and pepper.

4. Remove the melted cheese toasts from the broiler and slide onto
a plate. Using a spatula, place the egg, sunny-side up, on one
of the toasts. Top with the other cheese toast, cheese side down.
Eat immediately.

What Ya Got? SANDWICHES

A sandwich can be ordered in thousands of incarnations, with just as many names. The club, the grilled cheese, the egg salad, the PB & J, the BLT, the tuna melt, the French dip, panini, *báhn mì* . . . have all been inducted into in the Sandwich Hall of Fame. But have you ever sunk your teeth into a Sloppy Sussman Sammy?

My friends and coworkers will tell you: I'll *never* just call it a plain ol' sandwich. Every sandwich gets it own name, because I love, I *revere* sandwiches, and consider myself something of a sandwich connoisseur. Why do I maintain such a passionate love for the sandwich? Well, for one thing, I am an extremely fast eater, and so for me (and probably others like me), the "sandwich" is the most ingenious delivery method of tastiness to stomach ever created. Add to that high marks for versatility, convenience, and reliability, and the sandwich is arguably the most perfect food: highly transportable, often reheatable, always delicious. There is a reason the Egyptians had a hieroglyphic for sandwiches: because they worshipped them.

All of these sandwiches except one (the Liquored Up, an uninhibited improv) star leftovers from other recipes in this book, providing an opportunity to double down on your favorites. But there's no reason you shouldn't make the main recipe just to feed your sandwich love. Each sandwich here feeds one generously, or two if you want to cut it in half for a more moderate meal or a snack. —Eli

I'll NEVER just call it a plain ol' SANDWICH.

So you made biscuits with gravy, but the gravy is gone, or, for some insane reason, you don't feel like eating the gravy again. Let's get wild on those biscuits, right?

Buy some good-quality smoked salmon at a grocery store or deli. (This is also known as lox, if you are Jewish or live in a major metropolitan area.) About 2 oz (60 g) per biscuit will do nicely.

the SEABISCUIT

 FEATURING

BUTTERMILK BISCUIT (PAGE 21)
fresh dill, cream cheese, sea salt and pepper, lox

1. Slice the biscuit(s) open and warm in your toaster until golden brown. Meanwhile, mince some fresh dill very finely.

2. Spread softened cream cheese on both sides of each warm biscuit. Sprinkle each side with the dill and sea salt and pepper. Put a few slices of lox on the bottom half or halves. Close the sandwich(es) up and eat immediately.

The HOLY Schnitz

FEATURING

CHICKEN SCHNITZEL (PAGE 117)
mayonnaise, red onion, celery, red bell pepper, fresh rosemary, hot-pepper sauce, challah or sourdough, Dijon mustard and iceberg lettuce for serving

1. Take a leftover piece of schnitzel and cut it into ½-inch (12-mm) dice. Set aside.

2. In a bowl, combine ¼ cup (2 fl oz/60 ml) mayonnaise, ¼ cup (1 oz/30 g) thinly sliced red onion, ¼ cup (1 oz/30 g) finely diced celery, ¼ cup (1 oz/30 g) finely diced red bell pepper, 2 Tbsp minced fresh rosemary, and 2 Tbsp hot sauce. Stir to mix well, then gently fold in the schnitzel.

3. Serve the chicken schnitzel salad on toasted challah or sourdough bread with spicy Dijon mustard and crispy iceberg lettuce.

My roommate Kate likes to say that eating food is really just a good excuse for her to get a dose of Frank's RedHot Sauce. While I don't put it indiscriminately on every food item ever and dream about bathing in it like she does, it gives our chicken salad that Holy Schnitz kick. Don't mash this or drown it in mayo like a traditional chicken salad. You're not looking for the consistency of a Subway tuna sandwich here; the cubes stay intact. -Eli

THE Maccabi

FEATURING FRIED CHICKEN (PAGE 20) AND LATKES (PAGE 22)
Vegetable oil for frying, ketchup, sour cream, maple syrup, and/or herbs for topping

The only way to make a latke sandwich with fried chicken any more sacrilegious would be to name it after one of our people's greatest folk heroes. Take that, social tact!

So: You made latkes and fried chicken. (Wow, that brunch must have been epic. We salute you.) Let's go.

1. Put the fried chicken (1 meaty piece per sandwich does it) in a covered heatproof dish and reheat in a 350°F (180°C) oven until warm throughout, about 15 minutes. Uncover and bake for about 5 minutes longer to crisp up the skin. Remove from the oven and let cool slightly.

2. While the chicken is cooling, warm 1 Tbsp vegetable oil in a large frying pan over medium-high heat. Put 2 latkes in the pan and cook just to warm and brown, about 2 minutes per side. When the latkes are browned and sizzling, turn out onto a plate. Pull the chicken meat from the bones and place on top of one of the latkes. Be sure to get all that chicken-skin goodness in there, too.

3. You can top the sandwich with ketchup, sour cream with green onions or herbs, or even maple syrup, if you want to go all kinds of Roscoe's on this one. Put the other latke on top and eat immediately.

The TURKS and Caicos

FEATURING TURKISH BAKED EGGS (PAGE 30),
Sourdough bread, bacon and/or sausage

This sandwich is as delicious as its namesake islands are beautiful. And what's a Caribbean vacation about? Indulgence and extravagance. Same as this sandwich.

1. Put a couple of Turkish Baked Eggs with a scoop of sauce and spinach in a covered heatproof dish and reheat in a 350°F (180°C) oven until warm throughout, about 10 minutes. Meanwhile, get some rustic bread with a hearty crust. We suggest sourdough or a country boule.

2. If you've got bacon—awesome. If you've got sausage—even more awesome. Cut 1 sausage link in half lengthwise and fry it up in a large frying pan according to package directions, then set aside on paper towels. Fry 2 or 3 strips of bacon over medium-high heat until crispy, about 5 minutes. Set aside with the sausage.

3. Pour off all but about 1 Tbsp bacon grease from the pan and return the pan to medium-high heat. Fry 2 slices of bread in the bacon grease until nice and brown on both sides, about 1 minute per side. Turn them out onto a plate, slide the baked eggs with their sauce onto one piece, and pile on the sausage and bacon. Close the sandwich up and eat immediately.

> Yeah, this one's as dirty as it sounds. Christina Aguilera-level dirty. A triple-napkin type of sandwich. You'll need a baguette and some Parmesan cheese to pack up your leftovers into this delicious bag.

the SAUSAGE balls

 FEATURING → BAGUETTE, MEATBALLS FROM GRILLED MEATBALL SANDWICH (PAGE 43) AND MEAT RAGÙ (PAGE 80), Parmesan cheese

1. Preheat the broiler. Split any amount of baguette lengthwise and warm it in the oven while the broiler is heating up, just to toast it lightly, about 2 minutes.

2. Meanwhile, warm a few meatballs and a scoop of the ragù in a frying pan over medium-low heat. When they are piping hot, arrange the meatballs in a row on the bottom half of the baguette. Pour the ragù over the meatballs. Grate some Parmesan on top to cover generously. Slide under the broiler and broil just until the Parmesan melts and begins to bubble. Remove from the broiler, cover with the baguette top, and eat immediately.

SANDWICH TIPS

• You can grill any sandwich in a frying pan just by melting a little bit of butter over medium-high heat and applying your spatula. You do not need a celebrity grill or a panini press.

• Always have Dijon mustard in your fridge.

• Always have good-quality extra-virgin olive oil and a middle-priced balsamic vinegar in your pantry.

• A slice of tomato, as long as it's in season and ripe, makes nearly every sandwich better. So does cheese.

• Invest in good bread. A few more bucks makes the difference between a locally made fresh and delicious loaf and something that's spent five days frozen on a truck.

• Have your deli meat sliced for you at the deli counter. If it comes in a plastic shrink-wrapped package and the slices are all the exact same size, trust us, your sandwich will suck. Badly.

the Adam SANDLER
our version of a SLOPPY JOE

 FEATURING ➜ MEAT RAGÙ (PAGE 80), Worcestershire sauce, hot-pepper sauce, granulated garlic, salt and freshly ground pepper, baked beans (optional), bread of choice

1. Put a generous scoop of the ragù in a frying pan over medium heat and cook, stirring once in a while, until it's warm throughout and browned here and there, about 5 minutes.

2. Add 1 Tbsp Worcestershire sauce, 1 tsp hot-pepper sauce, 1 tsp granulated garlic, and a pinch each of salt and freshly ground pepper to the ragù. If you have a can of baked beans, add them to the pan. Stir often until the mixture comes to a simmer.

3. To function as the magic carpet for the ride to your mouth we suggest: onion rolls, hamburger buns, or toasted challah. Pile on the Joe (don't worry if it's sloppy) and eat immediately.

The LIQUORED Up

The classic Liquored Up sandwich consists of: small diced potatoes, panfried in butter or olive oil (get 'em crunchy); any kind of meat you can find in your fridge, but hopefully bacon is part of the equation (cook it crisp); any kind of cheese you have (but hopefully Cheddar or Swiss); ranch dressing (bottled okay); and hot sauce.

Wrap up all this deliciousness (to your taste) like a burrito in a flour tortilla and seal the whole thing shut in a hot frying pan greased with a spritz of cooking spray or 1 Tbsp butter or olive oil. Get everything melty and toasty, about 2 minutes per side. Eat immediately.

We had only six channels of TV growing up, so we watched a lot of Reading Rainbow. This sandwich is named after one of our favorite food books we saw on the show. Why we loved a book about a young boy who is forced to work in a butcher shop and then ends up turning into a fish is a bit troubling, as forced labor and turning into a fish don't usually rank high on little kids' to-do lists. But hey, at least we were reading, right? This sandwich is delicious but you don't have to take my word for it. —Eli

A NOTE ON BREAD

You'll see that every recipe here calls out specific bread suggestions for each sandwich. Still, whatever you've got around will probably do—unless it's processed white bread! If all you have in your pantry is bagged supermarket white bread, please run, don't walk, or get in your car and drive to the farmers' market/bakery/best supermarket nearest you and start buying baguettes, sourdough, challah, ciabatta, anything crusty, local, small-batch, or same-day baked . . . dear god, just start buying anything besides processed white bread. Your life will be richer. Spring for the good sh*t. Good bread makes all the difference.

the Louise THE FISH

FEATURING ➤ GRILLED WHOLE FISH (PAGE 53) OR BUTTER-POACHED COD (PAGE 69), cucumber, sour cream or yogurt, garlic, fresh dill, salt and freshly ground pepper, challah or sandwich roll, arugula

1. Peel a medium cucumber. Using a Microplane or box grater, grate the cucumber onto a clean kitchen towel. Wrap the towel around the grated cuke and squeeze gently to remove as much liquid as possible.

2. Put the cucumber in a bowl and add ½ cup (4 oz/125 g) sour cream or yogurt; 2 minced garlic cloves; 1 Tbsp minced fresh dill; and salt and freshly ground pepper to taste.

3. Spread the cut sides of 2 pieces of toasted challah or a split roll on one side with a generous helping of the cucumber sauce. (Use the remaining sauce for more Louise the Fishes.) Place a fish fillet on one half, put a few arugula leaves on top, close the sandwich, and eat immediately.

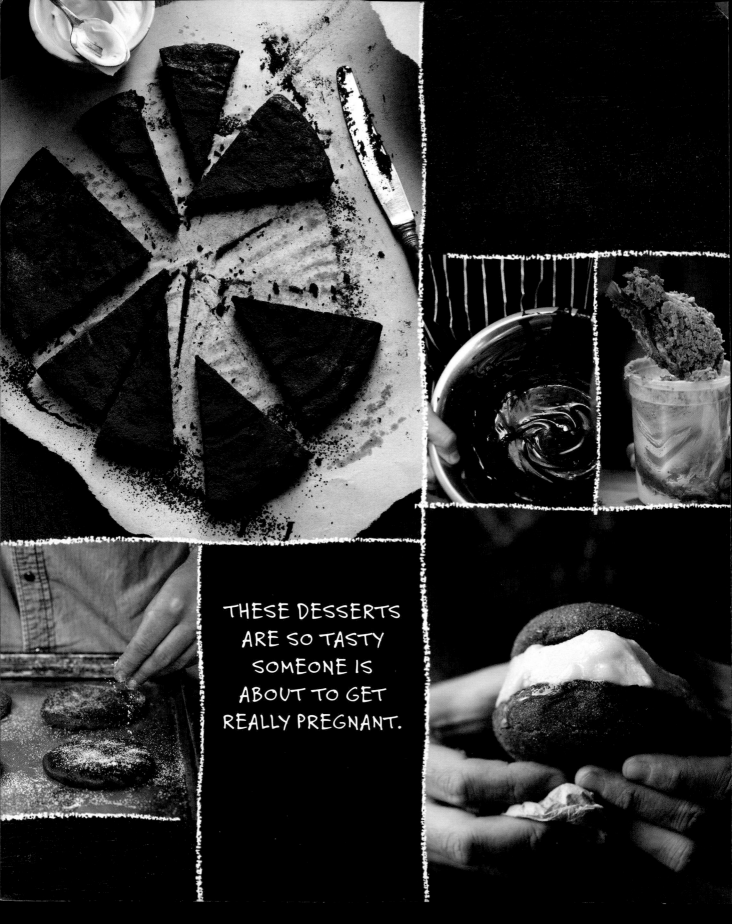

THESE DESSERTS
ARE SO TASTY
SOMEONE IS
ABOUT TO GET
REALLY PREGNANT.

Sweet Stuff

CHOCOLATE-PEANUT BUTTER PIE 142

FLOURLESS CHOCOLATE ESPRESSO TART 145

CEREAL CUPCAKES 146

SEASONAL GRANITAS 147

GINGERSNAP ICE-CREAM SANDWICHES 148

S'MORES WITH MAPLE-BOURBON MARSHMALLOWS 151

THIS IS A RECIPE WHERE WE TRIED TO CRAM AS MANY DELICIOUS INGREDIENTS AS WE COULD INTO A DESSERT THAT WOULD APPEAL TO SOMEONE WHO IS TERRIFIED ABOUT THE THOUGHT OF COMBINING FLOUR AND EGGS. IF YOU'RE CAPABLE OF READING THIS COOKBOOK, YOU ARE CAPABLE OF MAKING THIS DESSERT LOOK AS INSANELY GOOD AS THE PICTURE.

chocolate-peanut butter PIE

SERVES 6-8

3 CUPS (6 OZ/185 G) CRUMBLED GRAHAM CRACKERS

½ CUP (4 OZ/125 G) UNSALTED BUTTER, MELTED

1 CUP (6 OZ/185 G) SEMISWEET CHOCOLATE CHIPS

1 CUP (8 FL OZ/250 ML) HEAVY CREAM

½ CUP (1½ OZ/45 G) UNSWEETENED COCOA POWDER

½ CUP (4 OZ/125 G) CREAM CHEESE, AT ROOM TEMPERATURE

1 CUP (10 OZ/315 G) CRUNCHY PEANUT BUTTER, AT ROOM TEMPERATURE

1 CUP (5 OZ/155 G) SALTED PEANUTS, COARSELY CHOPPED

1. Preheat the oven to 375°F (190°C).

2. In a food processor, pulse the graham crackers until they are uniformly ground to the consistency of sand. Transfer to a bowl, add the melted butter, and stir to mix well. Grease a 9-inch (23-cm) pie tin and press the graham cracker mixture into the bottom, patting it into an even layer. Do not worry about covering the sides. Bake until golden brown, about 15 minutes. Remove from the oven and set aside to cool completely.

3. Put the chocolate chips in a large, heatproof bowl. In a small saucepan, heat the cream until just before it begins to boil. Pour the hot cream slowly over the chocolate chips while whisking constantly. Add the cocoa powder and whisk vigorously until the mixture is smooth. Place the chocolate sauce in the fridge while the crust is cooling.

4. In a small bowl, combine the cream cheese and peanut butter and beat with a wooden spoon until well blended. When the crust has cooled completely, using a rubber spatula, scrape the peanut butter–cream cheese filling into the crust and spread in a smooth, even layer. Drizzle the chocolate sauce over the top. Sprinkle the salted peanuts evenly over the top of the chocolate. Refrigerate until chilled, about 1 hour. Cut into wedges and serve right away.

HERE'S A PLAY OFF THE FLOURLESS CAKE OUR MOM USED TO MAKE FOR SPECIAL OCCASIONS. WE DECIDED TO ADD ESPRESSO TO GIVE IT ANOTHER KICK. YOU'LL BE SHOCKED HOW MOIST IT IS. IT'S SUPER DENSE AND RICH, IN BETWEEN FUDGE AND A BROWNIE.

flourless chocolate espresso TART

4 OZ (125 G) FINE-QUALITY BITTERSWEET CHOCOLATE

¾ CUP (6 OZ/185 G) SUGAR

½ CUP (4 OZ/125 G) UNSALTED BUTTER, MELTED AND COOLED TO ROOM TEMPERATURE

3 LARGE EGGS, LIGHTLY BEATEN

1 CUP (3 OZ/90 G) UNSWEETENED COCOA POWDER, PLUS MORE FOR DUSTING

1½ TBSP GROUND WHOLE ESPRESSO BEANS OR INSTANT ESPRESSO

WHIPPED CREAM (OPTIONAL)

1. Preheat the oven to 375°F (190°C). Butter an 8-inch (20-cm) round cake pan.

2. In the top pan of a double boiler, melt the chocolate over (but not touching) simmering water. Scrape the melted chocolate into a large bowl, add the sugar and melted butter, and stir to mix well. Add the eggs and mix well. Sift in the cocoa powder and espresso and stir until the batter is smooth and well blended. Pour into the prepared pan and bake until the top begins to form a fudge-like crust, 20–25 minutes.

3. Remove the cake from the oven and let cool in the pan for 10 minutes, then invert onto a serving plate. Dust with cocoa powder and top with whipped cream, if desired. Cut into wedges and serve right away.

I WAS HEADING TO A DINNER PARTY ONE NIGHT AND DIDN'T WANT TO COME EMPTY-HANDED OR WITH A LAME BOTTLE OF WINE. PROBLEM WAS, I DIDN'T HAVE THAT MANY GROCERIES AND BARELY ANY TIME AT ALL. THIS IS A PERFECT EXAMPLE OF LOOKING AT WHAT YOU HAVE AND MAKING SOMETHING GOOD WORK. TIP: IF YOU'RE SHORT ON SWEET TOPPINGS, RAID YOUR HOST'S FRIDGE FOR CHOCOLATE SAUCE, PB OR J, NUTS, OR ANY OTHER TOPPING YOU CAN GET YOUR HANDS ON. –ELI

MAKES 9 CUPCAKES

CEREAL CUPCAKES

2 CUPS (12 OZ/375 G) MAPLE OAT CLUSTERS AND FLAKES CEREAL (THINK HONEY BUNCHES OF OATS)

1 CUP (5 OZ/155 G) ALL-PURPOSE FLOUR

¼ CUP (2 OZ/60 G) PACKED LIGHT BROWN SUGAR

1 CUP (8 OZ/250 G) UNSALTED BUTTER, MELTED

1 LARGE EGG

VEGETABLE OIL COOKING SPRAY

FOR MAPLE-PECAN TOPPING

1¼ CUPS (5 OZ/155 G) CHOPPED PECANS

½ CUP (4 FL OZ/125 ML) PURE MAPLE SYRUP

½ CUP (4 OZ/120 G) PACKED BROWN SUGAR

1. Preheat the oven to 375°F (190°C).

2. Using a food processor (or by pressing the cereal between the bottom of a heavy bowl and a cutting board), crush the cereal until medium ground. Do not grind it to dust. Small chunks are fine.

3. In a large bowl, mix together the ground cereal, flour, and light brown sugar. Add the melted butter and egg and stir to blend well.

4. Spray 9 cupcake cups with a light coat of cooking spray. Press about ¼ cup (2 fl oz/60 ml) of the cupcake mix into each cupcake cup.

5. To make the maple-pecan topping, in a bowl, combine the pecans, maple syrup, and brown sugar. Stir to blend well and distribute over the cereal mixture so that each cup is filled to the top.

6. Bake the cupcakes until the tops turn golden brown, 12–15 minutes. Let the cupcakes cool on a wire rack, turn them out, and serve.

DO YOU LIKE THOSE FLAVORFUL ICE THINGS SERVED IN PAPER CONES? COOL. HERE IS A FANCY VERSION WITH A FANCIER NAME. TO SAVE PREP AND CLEANUP TIME WE REMOVED THE NEED FOR A BLENDER AND FRESH FRUIT, INSTEAD COMBINING FRUIT JUICE WITH OTHER TASTY FLAVORS. PUT YOUR SERVING BOWLS IN THE FREEZER FOR ABOUT TEN MINUTES BEFORE SERVING TO HELP KEEP THE GRANITA ICE-COLD AT THE TABLE. PAPER CONES SOLD SEPARATELY.

SERVES 4-6

seasonal GRANITAS

FOR LEMON-LIME GRANITA

3 CUPS (24 FL OZ/750 ML) LEMONADE MADE WITH 100% LEMON JUICE

ZEST OF 1 LEMON

ZEST OF 1 LIME

FOR APRICOT-GINGER GRANITA

3 CUPS (24 FL OZ/750 ML) 100% APRICOT JUICE

1 TBSP PEELED AND FINELY GRATED GINGER (USE A MICROPLANE IF POSSIBLE)

1. Pour the lemonade or apricot juice into a 9-by-13-inch (23-by-33-cm) metal or glass baking dish. You do not want the dish filled more than 1½ inches (4 cm) deep.

2. Add the lemon and lime zests to the lemonade or the ginger to the apricot juice. Stir to mix well. Place the dish in the freezer for 1 hour.

3. Remove the granita from the freezer and, using the tines of a fork, scrape the top layer to break up the ice. Return to the freezer for 1 hour longer. Repeat the scraping process. Continue this process at about 30-minute intervals until the granita is a nice mass of uniform ice shards, about 4–5 hours total. Scrape into serving bowls (or paper cones) and serve right away.

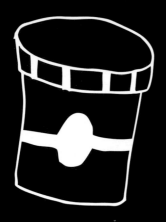

WE LOVE HOW GINGERSNAPS AREN'T THE TYPICAL COOKIE FLAVOR YOU'D EXPECT. OUR MOM HAS BEEN MAKING GINGERSNAP COOKIES FOR EVERY SINGLE GATHERING FOR AS LONG AS WE CAN REMEMBER. MAKING THIS RECIPE REMINDS US OF WHEN WE WERE KIDS. IN THIRTY MINUTES YOU'LL BE REMINISCING ABOUT YOUR OWN GOOD OLD DAYS WHILE MOWING DOWN ON ICE-CREAM SANDWICHES LIKE YOU'RE SIX AGAIN.

gingersnap

SERVES 4-6 ➡ ## ICE-CREAM SANDWICHES

2 CUPS (1 LB/500 G) SUGAR, PLUS MORE FOR ROLLING THE COOKIES

¾ CUP (6 OZ/185 G) SALTED BUTTER, MELTED

2 LARGE EGGS

½ CUP (5½ OZ/170 G) UNSULPHURED MOLASSES

½ TSP BAKING SODA

3 TSP GROUND GINGER

½ TSP GROUND CINNAMON

¼ TSP GROUND CLOVES

3½ CUPS (17½ OZ/545 G) ALL-PURPOSE FLOUR

1 PINT (14 OZ/440 G) BEST-QUALITY PEACH OR OTHER FLAVOR ICE CREAM, SLIGHTLY SOFTENED

1. Preheat the oven to 375°F (190°C).

2. In a large bowl, combine the 2 cups (1 lb/500 g) sugar and melted butter. Using a wooden spoon or rubber spatula, stir until thoroughly combined and smooth. Add the eggs and molasses and stir to mix well. Add the baking soda, ginger, cinnamon, and cloves and mix well. Add 2 cups (10 oz/315 g) of the flour and stir thoroughly until no flour can be seen in the mixture. Add the remaining 1½ cups (7½ oz/230 g) flour and stir until incorporated.

3. Pour sugar onto a plate. Form the dough into 12 balls about 2 inches (5 cm) in diameter. Roll each ball in the sugar to coat thoroughly, then place on a baking sheet. Bake until they just begin to crack on top, about 12 minutes. Remove from the oven and let cool for 2 minutes. Using a wide spatula, transfer to a wire rack to cool completely.

4. To assemble the ice-cream sandwiches, place 6 of the cookies, top sides down, on a work surface. Spoon about ⅓ cup (2½ oz/75 g) ice cream onto each, then top each with another cookie, top side up. Press gently to seal and to push the ice cream to the edges of the cookies. Serve right away.

WHEN IT CAME DOWN TO DEVISING THIS RECIPE, WE DETERMINED THE CENTERPIECE SHOULD BE, WELL . . . THE CENTER OF THE S'MORE. AND STORE-BOUGHT MARSHMALLOWS ARE TASTELESS BLOBS. ON OUR FIRST TRIAL RUN, WE CUT INTO THESE S'MORES AND EACH TOOK A HUGE BITE. WE LOOKED AT EACH OTHER AND SORT OF LOST OUR SHIT AT THE AWESOMENESS.

S'mores with MAPLE-bourbon marshmallows

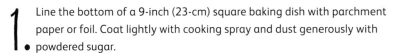

VEGETABLE OIL COOKING SPRAY (NOT OLIVE OIL)

POWDERED SUGAR FOR DUSTING

2 TBSP (TWO ¼-OZ/ 7-G ENVELOPES) UNFLAVORED GELATIN

¼ CUP (2 FL OZ/60 ML) BOURBON, PLUS 3 TBSP

¾ CUP (8 OZ/250 G) PURE MAPLE SYRUP

1½ CUPS (12 OZ/375 G) GRANULATED SUGAR

4 OZ (125 G) BITTERSWEET (60% CACAO) CHOCOLATE, CHOPPED

½ CUP (4 FL OZ/125 ML) HEAVY CREAM

9 GRAHAM CRACKERS, SNAPPED IN HALF

1. Line the bottom of a 9-inch (23-cm) square baking dish with parchment paper or foil. Coat lightly with cooking spray and dust generously with powdered sugar.

2. Pour ½ cup (4 fl oz/125 ml) warm water into a small bowl. Sprinkle the gelatin over and stir to dissolve.

3. In a saucepan over medium-high heat, combine the ¼ cup (2 fl oz/ 60 ml) bourbon, the maple syrup, and the granulated sugar. Bring to a boil and cook, stirring often, until the mixture registers 240°F (116°C) on a candy or deep-frying thermometer. Pour into the bowl of a stand mixer, if you have one. Add the dissolved gelatin and the remaining 3 Tbsp bourbon. Using the paddle attachment, beat until stiff peaks form when you lift the beaters out, 10–12 minutes. If you don't have a stand mixer, use a handheld mixer, but be sure to pour the hot syrup into a heatproof bowl for mixing, and be prepared for a little arm fatigue, as the beating time is substantial. Using a rubber spatula, scrape into the prepared dish and spread in an even layer to the edges of the pan. Let cool at room temperature until firm, about 4 hours.

4. Tip the marshmallow out of the pan and remove the lining. Trim ¾ inch (2 cm) off each edge, then cut into 9 squares. Sift a scoop of powdered sugar in a bowl, add the marshmallows, and toss to coat. Put the chocolate in a heatproof bowl. In a small saucepan over medium-high heat, warm the cream until just barely boiling. Meanwhile, arrange 9 of the graham cracker halves, top side down, on a baking sheet and place a marshmallow on top of each. Pour the hot cream over the chocolate and whisk until melted and smooth. Drizzle some of this melted chocolate mixture over each marshmallow, close the s'mores with another graham cracker half, and serve.

random stuff

that didn't fit anywhere else but is super f*cking delicious

FOR THE CHORIZO

1 lb (500 g) ground pork

6 garlic cloves, minced

1 Tbsp packed light brown sugar

1 Tbsp dried oregano

2½ tsp kosher salt

2 tsp smoked paprika

2 tsp ancho chile powder

1 tsp chipotle chile powder

1 tsp ground cumin

½ tsp ground coriander

½ tsp cayenne pepper

2 tsp red wine vinegar

1 Tbsp unsalted butter, if needed

¼ cup (1 1/2 oz/45 g) all-purpose flour

2 cups (16 fl oz/500 ml) whole milk

Chorizo Gravy

1. To make the chorizo, put the pork in a large bowl. Add all of the remaining chorizo ingredients and stir or use your hands to mix just until incorporated; you don't want to overwork the meat. Heat a small frying pan over medium heat. Pinch off a test patty of chorizo about the size of a 50-cent piece and place it in the hot pan. Cook, turning once, until no longer pink inside, about 3 minutes total. Taste and adjust the seasoning, if necessary.

2. Heat a saucepan over medium-high heat. Add the chorizo and cook, stirring to break up the meat, until nicely browned and cooked through, about 10 minutes. There should be a Tbsp or two of rendered fat in the pan. If there isn't, add the 1 Tbsp butter. Reduce the heat to medium. When the butter is melted (if using), add the flour and stir constantly for about 3 minutes to cook off the raw flour taste. Add the milk slowly and bring to a simmer. Reduce the heat to low and cook, stirring often, until thickened, about 3 minutes. Set aside and cover to keep warm. (You can make the chorizo gravy up to 2 days ahead of time. Cover tightly and store in the fridge. Reheat gently over medium-low heat before serving.)

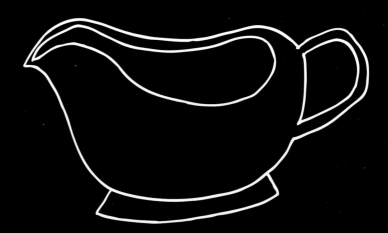

Thyme Spaetzle

1½ cups (7½ oz/235 g) all-purpose flour

Salt and freshly ground pepper

2 large eggs

¼ cup (2 fl oz/60 ml) half-and-half or whole milk

3 Tbsp unsalted butter

1 Tbsp minced fresh thyme

1. In a large bowl, combine the flour, 1 tsp salt, and ½ tsp pepper and stir to mix well. In a separate bowl, whisk together the eggs and half-and-half. Form a well in the dry ingredients and pour in the egg mixture. Stir the wet ingredients into the dry, gradually pulling the flour mixture into the well, and mix until the dough is smooth. Let the dough rest at room temperature for 20 minutes.

2. Bring a pot of generously salted water to a boil over high heat. Take up a large slotted spoon. Pull off a portion of the dough and, using the back of a soupspoon, push it through the holes or slots of the large spoon into the boiling water. Repeat 2 times for one batch of spaetzle; you don't want to crowd the pot. When the spaetzle float to the surface, scoop them out, transfer to a colander placed in the sink, and rinse quickly under cool running water. Repeat to cook the remaining dough.

3. When all of the spaetzle has been boiled and rinsed, melt the butter in a large frying pan over medium heat. When the butter is hot and foamy, add the spaetzle and stir to coat evenly. Stir in the thyme. Sauté the spaetzle until they begin to brown and crisp slightly, 1–2 minutes. Serve right away.

Apple Chutney

1 Tbsp olive oil

2 white onions, chopped

3 apples, cored and roughly chopped

¼ cup (2 oz/60 g) packed light brown sugar

1 Tbsp peeled and chopped fresh ginger

1 tsp ground allspice

Zest and juice of ½ lemon

Salt

1. In a frying pan, heat the olive oil over medium heat. Add the onions and stir to coat with the oil. Reduce the heat to low and cook, stirring often, until the onions are caramelized to a deep golden brown, about 45 minutes.

2. Put the apples in a saucepan and add ¼ cup (2 fl oz/60 ml) water. Simmer over low heat until very tender, about 30 minutes. Mash the apples, but leave some nice chunky texture.

3. Add the onions, brown sugar, ginger, allspice, lemon zest and juice, and a pinch of salt to the pan with the apples and stir to mix well. Serve warm or at room temperature.

Shiitake Broth

8 cups (64 fl oz/2 l)
good-quality, low-sodium
chicken broth

4 oz (125 g) fresh
shiitake mushrooms,
stemmed and diced

4 green onions,
white and tender
green parts only, sliced

2 Tbsp peeled and
roughly chopped
fresh ginger

1. In a soup pot, combine the chicken broth, green onions, shiitakes, and ginger. Bring to a boil over medium-high heat, stirring occasionally, then cover partially and reduce the heat to maintain a very low simmer; let simmer for about 15 minutes.

Arugula Pesto

½ cup (2 oz/60 g)
walnut pieces

½ cup (2 oz/60 g)
freshly grated
Parmesan cheese

1 garlic clove, minced

Kosher salt

2 cups (2 oz/60 g)
packed arugula
leaves

1 cup (8 fl oz/250 ml)
extra-virgin olive oil

1. In a food processor, combine the walnuts, garlic, arugula, Parmesan, and 1 tsp salt and pulse to blend. With the machine running, pour in the olive oil through the food tube in a slow, steady stream and process until smooth, stopping to scrape down the sides of the bowl as needed. Taste and adjust the seasonings.

Spicy Aioli

2 large egg yolks

½ tsp kosher salt

2 Tbsp apple cider
vinegar

½ tsp cayenne pepper

¼ tsp paprika

1 garlic clove, minced

½ tsp Dijon mustard

1 cup (8 fl oz/250 ml)
extra-virgin olive oil

1. In a food processor, combine the egg yolks, vinegar, garlic, mustard, salt, cayenne, and paprika and pulse to blend. With the machine running, pour in the olive oil through the food tube in a slow, steady stream until the mixture is thick and emulsified. Taste and adjust the seasonings.

Za'atar

3 Tbsp sumac

1 Tbsp coriander seeds

2 Tbsp fresh thyme

2 tsp coarse sea salt

2 Tbsp dried oregano

1 Tbsp ground cumin

1 Tbsp fennel seed

1. Grind all the ingredients in a spice grinder or using a mortar and pestle. Store in an airtight container for up to 6 months.

sea salt

INDEX

DISCARDED

thank you

MAX SUSSMAN

My folks: What can one say to the most supportive and encouraging parents one could ask for? Thanks for always being on my side. Carlo: My time at Roberta's working with you has made me continually refine and improve my idea of quality, creativity, and what good food means to me, which I hope is reflected in this cookbook. I want to thank you for not only allowing but encouraging me to pursue this project while at Roberta's. It's been the most interesting 2 years of my life. Everybody from Roberta's: What an amazing crew of beautiful weirdos! I love you all. And especially the kitchen crew: I rarely get teary eyed but sometimes when I think of all of you I think of Captain Picard talking to the Enterprise crew when he went back in time in Part II of "All Good Things" and told them they were the best crew he'll ever work with, but they didn't really know who he was yet, but he knew how awesome they were. Great episode. Stay hydrated please. Alex, Ben, Eisha, Erica, Kate, Mark, Rachel, Evan, Lulu & Ben: Thanks for looking so good while you so very very slowly ate our food. Kate: To the person who has been here through it all, to whose advice I know I should always listen to, thank you for everything. April: Working with you, even briefly, was one of the most educational experiences I've ever had. What I absorbed from you I know will stay with me forever. Alison: Thanks to you and your crew for initiating us into the secrets of food styling. We'll never look at a spray bottle or mini torch the same way again.

ELI SUSSMAN

Ema and Abba: Thanks for each side of my brain, the artistic and the analytical; for my inherited skillfulness in everything from swearing to list making; for making me into a leader among men; for everything that's happened and for everything that will happen—thank you. Max: To my partner in crime and the best teacher and mentor a young cook and brother could ever have. Another cookbook under our belt and I actually don't want to kill you. Kate: Thanks for being that pesky sister who isn't afraid to tell me I am an idiot giving feedback (always giving feedback…) and for your glamorous modeling work inside. Max Aronson: You tell it like it is and

I will always need that. I'm sorry I always got drunk and fell asleep while cooking things when we lived together. Sam, Michael & Matt: I could not ask for better teachers. Tapping into your brains and learning from you all is the greatest gift NYC has given me. Noah and Rae: A guy can't ask for better, more supportive bosses. Thanks for inviting me into the family with such open arms. Joy, Judy & Christine: Thanks for everything I learned from you with TOTNLA!

FROM MAX AND ELI

Nana and Papa: We would never have been able to accomplish the things we do without the incredibly supportive family that you lead. Thanks for being firmly behind us every step of the way. Aunts and uncles cousins: You are all incredible! Thanks for buying 20 copies each (ok 50! sure 100!) and testing recipes (and not getting annoyed when all we talk about is food). Recipe testers: We couldn't have finished and revised these without all of you who took your time and money to help us make these deliciously usable recipes. Williams-Sonoma: Thank you for the opportunity. We do not take it lightly how much time and effort so many wonderful WS employees have invested into making this project a successful reality. We are honored to be involved with such a wonderful company. We hope we did all of you very proud. Ali, Amy, Hannah & Gonzalo: We'd be lost without you and the Weldon Owen team. Without you this book would read: welcum to a ckbooke by Maxi and Elie Sussmane, We luv cook food tasty town." And also, it would look like shit and never have gotten finished. For your expertise, guidance, and above all—your patience—you deserve several large cocktails mixed by us. Alex: All we asked is that you make us look in the book 50% as handsome as you do in real life. Mission accomplished sir, mission accomplished. Eric Rayman, our lawyer: Thanks for negotiating the contracts. We typed these thank yous on our jewel-encrusted ipads from our private yacht in St. Tropez. So yeah, you did a real bang up job. Jean Armstrong: You believed in us and spent a year fighting for us to get this book made. From the first meeting to every time we exchange emails, the enthusiasm and your ability to just get things done is contagious and inspiring.

Olive Press
Recipes and text © Copyright 2012 Eli Sussman and Max Sussman
Images and illustrations © Copyright 2012 Weldon Owen, Inc.
All rights reserved, including the right of reproduction in whole or in part in any form
Olive Press is an imprint of Weldon Owen, Inc. and Williams-Sonoma, Inc.
Weldon Owen, Inc. is a division of Bonnier Corporation
415 Jackson Street, Suite 200, San Francisco, CA 94111

Library of Congress Control Number: 2012934052

ISBN 978-1-61628-214-1

www.weldonowen.com
www.williams-sonoma.com

Printed and bound in China by Toppan-Leefung Printers Limited

First printed in 2012
10 9 8 7 6 5 4 3